INDIANA BREWERIES

INDIANA BREWERIES

JOHN HOLL & NATE SCHWEBER

STACKPOLE
BOOKS

The authors and the publisher encourage readers to visit the breweries and sample their beers, and recommend that those who consume alcoholic beverages
travel with a designated nondrinking driver.

Printed in the United States of America

10 9 8 7 6 5 4 3 2 1

FIRST EDITION

Cover design by Tessa J. Sweigert

Labels and logos are used with permission from the breweries

Library of Congress Cataloging-in-Publication Data

Holl, John.
    Indiana breweries / John Holl & Nate Schweber. — 1st ed.
        p.   cm.
    Includes index.
    ISBN-13: 978-0-8117-0661-2 (pbk.)
    ISBN-10: 0-8117-0661-3 (pbk.)
    1. Bars (Drinking establishments)—Indiana—Guidebooks. 2. Micro-
breweries—Indiana—Guidebooks. 3. Breweries—Indiana—Guidebooks.
    I. Schweber, Nate. II. Title.
    TX950.57.I6H65   2011
    663'.309772—dc22
                                                        2010050872

To my wife, April Darcy
Because the best part of all my beer-related travel is coming home to you
JH

To my Grandad Norman Schweber
Who always wanted me to write a book
And to my Grandpa Robert A. Vinci
Who surely would have
approved of the subject matter
NS

Contents

Foreword   ix
Acknowledgments   xiii
Introduction   1

Chicagoland and the Great Lakes: Northern Indiana   15

Crown Brewing   18
3 Floyds Brewing Company   21
Mishawaka Brewing Company   24
Figure Eight Brewing   26
Back Road Brewery   28
Shoreline Brewery & Restaurant   30
A Word About . . . Beer Travel   34

The Hoosier Heartland: Central Indiana and Fort Wayne   37

People's Brewing Company   40
Mad Anthony Brewing Company   43
Lafayette Brewing Company   45
Half Moon Restaurant & Brewery   48
Barley Island Brewing Company   51
Big Woods Brewing Company   53
Wilbur BrewHause   55
New Boswell Brewing Company   57
Oaken Barrel Brewing Company   60
Black Swan Brewpub   61
Three Pints Brewing   63
Heorot   65
A Word About . . . Brewing Beer   66

Crossroads of America: Indianapolis   69

Brugge Brasserie   74
Alcatraz Brewing Company   76

Ram Restaurant & Brewery 77
Sun King Brewery 80
Broad Ripple Brewpub 82
Rock Bottom Restaurant & Brewery, Downtown 84
Rock Bottom Restaurant & Brewery, College Park 86
Upland Tasting Room 88
Scotty's Thr3e Wise Men Brewing Company 89
Triton Brewing Company 91
Flat12 Bierwerks 92
The Bier Brewery and Taproom 94
A Word About . . . The Hoosier State 96

More Than Just a College Town: Bloomington 99

Lennie's/Bloomington Brewing Company 102
Upland Brewing Co. 104
A Word About . . . Made in Indiana 107

Uplands and Ohio River: Southern Indiana 111

Power House Brewing Company 114
Great Crescent Brewery 117
The New Albanian Brewing Company Pizzeria & Public House 119
The New Albanian Brewing Company Bank Street Brewhouse 121
Turoni's Main Street Brewery 123

Beerwebs 125
Glossary 127
Index 138

Foreword

In a world driven by cutting-edge technologies, I've managed to retain certain Luddite proclivities even while conceding ground to my iPhone and laptop.

When I get home after a long day of professional beer drinking, I empty my pockets of small change, a smudged Sharpie, and my trusty cigar cutter. Customarily there are various scrawlings on little paper scraps, magazine subscription cards, package store sales receipts, and crusty, beer-soaked coasters.

On a groggy, grumpy weekday morning some months back, a cursory examination of one of these reminders revealed this unintelligibility: "Jahnenollbeerbk."

After two espressos and some appropriate reflection, the translation finally took shape amid the haze: Yes, of course, it was that pleasant fellow at the pub from New Jersey, asking me questions about the brewery as the empty pints snaked down the bar's surface like so many glass dominoes waiting to fall and break my liver.

John Holl, right, and the book he was writing with some guy named Nate. Check.

Wait: a book about Indiana beer. Imagine that!

Hailing from Indiana, otherwise known as the Hoosier State, means living as a stereotype. We're supposed to be basketball-loving, soybean-growing, corn-shucking devotees of the Indianapolis 500, inhabiting flat ground somewhere in the vicinity of Illinois, drinking oceans of ice-cold, low-calorie, light golden lager after putting up hay, or downing boilermakers before shifts at doomed rust belt factories, all of which are both true and false, just like all stereotypes.

Hoosiers may not fully understand the meaning of the word "Hoosier," but one element of our Indiana experience appears to be stealth, at least as it pertains to beer and brewing. Almost unnoticed, three dozen breweries (and more on the way) have settled into their joyous daily routines in Indiana communities large and small, from Indianapolis to Nashville, and from Fort Wayne to Aurora.

It didn't seem possible two decades ago, when we'd lash steamer trunks to our hand-cranked, Indiana-made Studebaker and make the long muddy drive from New Albany, through waist-deep potholes and past extensive herds of free-range bison, all the way to Indianapolis, the state capital, eager to experience real beer at Broad Ripple Brewing Company.

It was the state's very first brewpub, and members of the Brewers of Indiana Guild annually honor founder John Hill's birthday by thanking him for his admirable prescience, not to mention patience.

We didn't call it craft beer in those ancient times. We simply called it good beer, and I believe I knew the name, rank, and serial number of every person in the state who shared my preference for it.

At times it was a lonely existence, just me and a few of my closest friends, like Fidel and Che camped in the Sierra Maestra mountains, sifting through the flotsam and jetsam of mass-produced, carbonated alco-pop in search of the stray hop, all the while watching the yokels flee in terror at the mere sight of "the dark stuff."

Twenty years later, we're still a minority, but good beer—craft beer—is accepted and available in Indiana as never before. In this book, John and Nate tell you where to find the Hoosier breweries and drink the beer they brew, and also other prime locations for craft and just plain good beer from America and all over the world. Never again will you be obliged to grudgingly accept the paltry selections at that familiar chain restaurant's bar.

Instead, like the authors themselves, you'll be meeting the regulars at the Heorot in Muncie, or drinking world-renowned ale at the 3 Floyds taproom in Munster, or while in Evansville, choosing the perfect beer to accompany pizza at Turoni's. John and Nate cannot magically render you into the most interesting man (or woman) in the world. They do, however, provide complete instructions on how to drink the most interesting beer in Indiana, thus lessening America's dependence on foreign Dos Equis and immeasurably enhancing the pleasure when the Colts once again defeat the Patriots.

This Hoosier journey in pursuit of better beer is noteworthy because it simultaneously validates Indiana's historic and cultural nineteenth-century virtues—think of John Wooden, the late iconic basketball legend who grew up in Martinsville—while pointing the way forward to twenty-first-century goals like artisanal integrity, local sourcing, and environmental sustainability. Most small brewers were going back to the future, green and local, before the buzzwords started trending.

Just ask Clay Robinson, Sun King's advocate of recyclable cans; or Jeff Mease, organic farmer, water buffalo rancher, and owner of Bloomington Brewing Company; or the pioneering Abstons, who are building trellises and growing hops in the hilly knobs that rise above the Ohio River in Floyd County.

My favorite single aspect of being in the brewing business in Indiana, and by extension, the reason why the brewing business is the best business in America, is that all of us are like family.

Greg Emig brewed for John Hill at Broad Ripple Brewing and then moved on to found Lafayette Brewing Company. Chris Johnson brewed for Greg and now is the owner-brewer at People's Brewing. Ted Miller also brewed for John before leaving to sell and install brewing systems worldwide. Ted returned to Indianapolis to open Brugge Brasserie, and today Kevin Matalucci, Ted's high school classmate, is two blocks away from Brugge up the Monon Trail, brewing beer for John at Broad Ripple Brewing, as he has done since Ted left.

Indiana craft brewing is community, not competitive. We cooperate, not connive. It's family. On those mercifully rare occasions when a brewery goes out of business, we lament and console the survivors, while advising and assisting the next wave. It's a tall order, but we're working together to put Indiana-brewed beer in the hands of the many Hoosiers who've yet to experience it.

In this book, John Holl and Nate Schweber do more than document the Indiana beer and brewing scene. They convey an overall sense of our brewing community and its ethos. John and Nate came to our places, drank our pints (samples just don't tell the tale), walked the walk, stumbled the stumble, and deciphered the cryptic notes the next morning while searching for Advil in a hotel room on the wrong side of the interstate.

Read, enjoy, and start planning your trip to Indiana. We Hoosiers have the ideal brew waiting, whatever your taste.

—Roger A. Baylor
Publican, New Albanian Brewing Company and
Board Member, Brewers of Indiana Guild

Acknowledgments

Ours was a friendship forged in beer. As young reporters in New Jersey we first met in 2005 over pints of Guinness in Jersey City. From there our friendship has taken us around the United States and out of the country. Along the way, we met many interesting people, shared laughs and good times with friends and family and, of course, had our fair share of beer.

As journalists, we've written about everything from crime and politics to culture and sports. Writing about beer seemed the next natural step. Sincere thanks go to Kyle Weaver at Stackpole Books, who approved our idea, offered encouragement, and expertly shepherded us through what can be a sometimes frustrating but ultimately rewarding experience.

This book is based on previous guidebooks in the Stackpole series, pioneered by Lew Bryson. Thus far, he has written the definitive beer guides to Pennsylvania, New York, New Jersey, and Virginia, Maryland, and Delaware. Always a gentleman, Lew shared his wisdom with us via email as we crisscrossed around the Hoosier Heartland and gave us hope when this book seemed like it would never be completed. Early on, Lew shared a piece of information that while simple, proved to be invaluable. We hope you will heed it as well: "Drink plenty of water, and never pass up an opportunity to urinate."

Mark Haynie, Paul Ruschmann, and Maryanne Nasiatka have also written brewery guidebooks for Stackpole and our thanks go to them as well for sharing war stories, tips, and memories. Bryce Eddings, our beer journalist colleague whose *Missouri Breweries* book should be soon hitting the shelves, was a great resource for sharing ideas as our deadlines came down to the wire. We stood on the shoulders of great writers and editors and are thankful for their support and guidance.

We worked together for the *New York Times* and owe a tremendous amount of thanks to the reporters and editors who shaped our careers and helped hone our skills: Mary Ann Giordano, Robert D. McFadden, John Harney, Robert Hanley, Michael Wilson, Jim Dwyer, Dan Barry, Patrick Farrell, Anthony Ramirez, and countless others.

We were also privileged to work with a great and inspiring man, Dith Pran, who until his death in 2008 shared his story of survival against the Khmer Rouge during the Cambodian genocide. He never missed an opportunity to inform classrooms, civic groups, or anyone else who would listen about the struggles in his native land. His legacy lives on in all who knew him and heard his story.

Several years ago, we met a Staten Island native who goes by the name of Mark J. Bonamo. A unique and passionate fellow who has more mojo than just about anyone we know, Mark has been a constant source of merriment, YouTube clips, and quirky sayings. His contributions to his book and our lives are immense, and he forever has our respect and thanks.

While in Indiana we relied on the kindness of family, friends, brewers, and native Hoosiers for everything from a comfortable place to sleep to a warm meal and tips on must-see attractions and can't-miss bars. In particular we thank Kelly and Brian Hage, Jon Murray, John Strauss, Ruth Holladay, Jen Wagner, Vic Ryckaert, Tom Spalding, John Fritze, Kristina Buchthal, Tosha Daugherty, Betsy Perry Paton, Laura Libs, Ted Miller, Roger A. Baylor, Jared Williamson, Ed Needham, Jason Tredo, David and Beth Howard, Jack Frey, Dave Colt, Clay Robinson, Steve Koers, Bob Ostrander, Sylvia Halladay, Kevin Corcoran, and Marie Walsh.

—*J.H.* and *N.S.*

Thanks to my father, John, who has always led by example, who taught me the value of the written word, and whose love, encouragement, and wide, welcoming smile has shaped my life and spurred me on these last three decades.

On the family front, I thank my stepmother Carolyn, mother-in-law Teresa Darcy, dear friend Ray Schroth, and my aunts and uncles, who have supported my efforts all my life.

My siblings Tom, Bill, Dan, Amanda, and brother-in-law Todd (a Wisconsin native who would send, on a near daily basis, beer-themed articles from his home state that served as a welcome distraction from everyday work) make life better and continually filled with good conversation and laughs.

My friends Joseph Biland, Joseph Gregov, Erick and Jamie Lawson, John Bonanni, Michael Alfonzo, Nick Mistretta, Michele de Oliveria, Steve and Kathy Sandberg, Levon Putney, Katie Zezima, and Dave Shaw are always good company to share a few pints and long stories with. They make this world a little brighter.

A tip of the hat to the Union County prosecutor, Theodore J. Romankow, who was generous with giving me time off from my full-time job to work on this very rewarding project. He is a source of professional encouragement and everyone should be lucky enough to have a boss like him.

Around the time of my twenty-first birthday, my friend Marc Cregan signed me up for a craft beer of the month club. That gift led me to the Gaslight Restaurant and Brewery in South Orange, New Jersey, where I had my first microbrew on draft and where the Soboti family and bartender Jeff Levine have continually supplied me with well-made session beers and hearty food. They helped begin this beer journey, should anyone be looking to cast blame.

There are several publications that continually publish my articles on craft beer and the culture of drinking, and for that I'd like to thank Nick Kaye and Lynn Davis at *Beer Connoisseur* magazine, Andy Lagomarsino at *New Jersey Newsroom*, Vince Capano at BeerNexus.com, Tony Forder at the *Ale Street News*, and Julia Herz at craftbeer.com

Although my part of the book is dedicated to my wife April Darcy, she deserves additional praise. She is my best friend, my muse, and a constant source of happiness. She was incredibly patient during this process but it couldn't have been accomplished without her.

—J.H.

My infamous 1999 Chevy Cavalier would have been junked and towed long ago were it not for the alchemic mechanical skills and watchful eye of Matt Popola and his extended family at Paddy's Service Station in Newark.

Enormous thanks to my friend and Midwestern musical comrade Dan McGuinness for lodging and rock 'n' roll gigs. Also huge thanks to my cousin Brad Thornton and his bride Courtney Reesor, who put me up for a few days in Kokomo, Indiana, along with their excitable poodle Layla and a bunny rabbit that I was introduced to as Princess Grace, but who now, after an examination by the vet, goes by the name Elvis. Appreciation to my old friend Jonathan Stanley, who I hadn't seen in fifteen years but put me up for a night and gave me a tour of the church organ he plays in Madison, Indiana.

Thanks to my Nana and Grandad, Mavis and Norman Schweber, for Chicagoland lodging and love. Thanks to my stepfather Bill Innes for Montana brews and camping. Biggest thanks to my Smurfette, Kristen Couchot. Thanks to my family: Phil Schweber, Kay Vinci, Gig Schweber, Carolyn Schweber, Erin Schweber, Andrew Schweber, and Sam Innes.

—N.S.

Introduction

Back home again in Indiana,
And it seems that I can see
The gleaming candlelight, still shining bright,
Through the sycamores for me.
The new-mown hay sends all its fragrance
From the fields I used to roam.
When I dream about the moonlight on the Wabash,
Then I long for my Indiana Home
  —*"(Back Home Again in) Indiana"*
    by Ballard MacDonald and James F. Hanley

It can be easy to overlook the beer offerings of the Hoosier state, not because Indiana breweries are not producing world-class beers; they are. It's because Indiana as a state is often overlooked as a whole. Take the national weather map for example. When it comes to that section of the Midwest, Chicago is always clearly marked. Same goes for Cincinnati. The 35,866 square miles between Illinois and Ohio rarely gets the love.

Indiana, however, deserves a closer look, not just because it has given us the likes of David Letterman, Orville Redenbacher, and John Mellencamp, or because of the Colts, the 500, and great college athletics.

No, it deserves a look because of the beer. It is no longer fair to assume that all great American craft beer comes from Vermont, Colorado, or the Pacific Northwest. While we all were busy scooping up the offerings from Stone, Avery, Full Sail, Dogfish Head, and other well-known craft breweries, Indiana brewers were flying under the radar and serving beers that you could only get if you lived inside the borders.

But respect is coming to Indiana beer. At the 2010 World Beer Cup in Chicago, five Indiana breweries—Sun King, Upland, 3 Floyds, Rock Bottom, and Crown Brewing—received honors out of 3,330 entries. You'll read about those establishments, and many more, in the pages that follow.

History Of Brewing In The United States

History tells us that the Pilgrims, the folks who left England to escape religious persecution, actually landed at Plymouth Rock because they were running low on beer—well, beer and other supplies, plus the

Mayflower got pretty banged up in the voyage across the Atlantic. The original plan was to land in Virginia, but they settled in Massachusetts instead. Regardless, beer played an important role in our history.

By the time George Washington was elected president of the new nation, cider was the preferred fermented beverage. Rum was popular as well. There were still imported beers from the Old World that were consumed, mostly ales, but the young country was far from the beer-consuming nation it is today.

In the mid-1840s, as German immigrants began coming to the United States, they brought with them centuries of brewing tradition and knowhow. Breweries began popping up in cities from Philadelphia to Milwaukee. Lager was the clear favorite for brewers to produce and customers to consume. Beer became so popular and demand so great that by 1900 there were roughly two thousand breweries in the country.

Businesses like Best's Brewing Company of Milwaukee (which would later become Pabst) and Anheuser-Busch of St. Louis grew large while others remained small, and others simply fell by the wayside.

All this drinking, however, upset some folks in the Temperance movement, and in 1920 they were able to push through a plan that resulted in a thirteen-year nightmare called Prohibition. Some brewers were able to stay afloat by selling sodas or near-beer, a low-alcohol alternative that compromised on ingredients and seriously damaged flavors. By the time Prohibition was repealed in 1933, there were few breweries left standing. In fact, by the 1960s, there were only about forty breweries left in the country. Most of these were large and controlled the market. Only a few regional breweries survived. Mostly, however, what was on the shelves and on tap was from the big breweries like Anheuser-Busch, and the beer was watered-down light lager, a far cry from the brewing heyday just seven decades earlier.

Modern-Day Craft

With only a handful of breweries left in the United States, options were slim for someone looking for a beer beyond the pale remains of the once-proud lagers brewed in the East and in the Midwest. One of breweries that had survived was Anchor Brewing of San Francisco, but the books were in nearly as bad shape as the structure itself. Enter Fritz Maytag, of the appliance manufacturing family, who enjoyed the flavorful ales produced by Anchor and used some of his fortune to purchase and rehab the brewery in the 1960s. He brought it back from the brink and turned it into one of the great American craft breweries. Maytag actually held onto the brewery until last year, when he sold it to a group of investors.

But Anchor was already a modest-sized brewery when Maytag took over. It would take a scrappy, determined, and some might say crazy individual to start a brewery from scratch.

That person would wind up being Jack McAuliffe, who launched the New Albion Brewing Company in Sonoma, California, in 1976. What today would seem like an ordinary act of entrepreneurism was revolutionary back then. To open a brewery, like McAuliffe did, with an annual capacity was just 450 barrels a year was unheard of.

Furthermore, the equipment to brew that little amount was extremely hard to come by. So, using his engineering background, McAuliffe got down to work, salvaged old dairy equipment, and welded together the rest to create a working brewery.

The beer was a hit—at least around Sonoma and California's Bay Area—and people would come long distances to try this new "micro beer." The demand was there, but ultimately the funding was not. When McAuliffe needed capital to keep the brewery afloat, banks were reluctant to give him a loan. They looked at him, McAuliffe would later recall, like he was from Mars and speaking Martian. So, just five years after opening, McAuliffe was forced to close. His equipment went north to Mendocino Brewing, one of many that would open in New Albion's wake, and McAuliffe quit the brewing business all together, moving around the country and eventually settling in Texas.

To this day, McAuliffe disclaims himself as a pioneer, dismissing any potential impact his brewery had on the American craft beer movement. But for those who knew him and were inspired by him, his impact was undeniable.

Ken Grossman, who was running a homebrew supply shop in Chico, California, around the time McAuliffe opened New Albion, visited the small brewery and realized that he too could open his own place. Today, Sierra Nevada Brewing Company is the second largest craft brewery in America, according to the Brewer's Association, a trade group that monitors the craft beer industry. McAuliffe, Grossman, and others who opened in the late 1970s and early 1980s largely had homebrewers to thank. When homebrewing became legal, many who had already been doing it on the down-low tried their hand at going pro. Those who didn't make the leap supported their local breweries and spurred them on, enhancing the bottom line and bringing new people to the fold. The homebrewers are a fervent lot and they continue to inspire and in many cases become the craft brewers that we know today.

There have been peaks and valleys since McAuliffe first opened his brewery. The mid-1990s saw a glut of breweries open up, some carrying names of animals, various bodily functions, or names that were borderline offensive. These breweries, playing off the public's new-found interest in craft, were good for a consumer laugh, but the product inside the bottles was lacking and a once-bitten consumer was too shy to go back.

Those that survived generally thrived. This second generation of brewers did things right, correctly marketing their brands and going for extreme beers with high alcohol content and strong hop flavor, playing into a niche of mostly younger beer drinkers who wanted to break away from their parents' beers. Some examples include Delaware's Dogfish Head Brewery and Pennsylvania's Victory Brewing.

Breweries opened and closed, some changed ownership, but things in the craft mostly remained static for a while as people settled into a world with craft beer. Then at the late part of the last decade the industry began to see things ramp up again. A lot of this, strangely enough, can be attributed to the recession. Avid homebrewers, laid off from their weekly nine-to-five jobs, took this as a sign to follow their dreams and open a brewery. Funding, still easier to secure than it was for McAuliffe, has been available, and today it seems there are breweries opening in every town. The Brewer's Association recently released a figure that indicates the majority of Americans now live within ten miles of a brewery. That's not tough to imagine when you consider that in the craft arena alone, there are more than sixteen hundred micro-breweries and brewpubs in the United States. That's the highest number since Prohibition ended in 1933.

Indiana, as you will see, has a modest but growing amount. This can only mean good things for thirsty Hoosiers and travelers to the state. But it's been a long road for Indiana and its breweries. To appreciate where we are today, we must first take a look back.

History of Beer in Indiana

Picture a chart of Indiana's breweries through the ages like this: Imagine someone—the St. Pauli Girl perhaps—climbing to the top of a waterslide, sliding back down, skimming just above the ground, and then flying back up a ramp.

If it helps, imagine the pool is filled with beer.

The climb starts in 1816, months before Indiana was even a state, when the territory's first amber waves of grain were transformed into amber beverage.

The slide begins in the late 1800s, courtesy of prohibitionists, when the number of Hoosier beer breweries numbered near ninety. Four decades later, even before the Eighteenth Amendment, there wasn't a single one brewing beer.

The return came slowly. When the Twenty-First Amendment repealed Prohibition and the Great Depression sandbagged the nation, a few breweries that survived by brewing soft drinks returned to the real stuff. They were then ravaged by the onslaught of the corporate brewery, its refrigerated railcars, and its smothering advertising budget. By 1960, there were only four breweries remaining in Indiana, all of them former family-owned businesses that had sold out to big corporations. Twenty years later, there were just two.

Then the jump. The state's remarkable beer renaissance began in the early 1990s when the legislature hopped on the burgeoning national microbrewing trend blowing east from the Pacific coast. Indiana legalized brewpubs. The next two decades saw more than fifty breweries blossom, more than Indiana had seen in the past century.

"Indiana has a really interesting brewing history," says historian Bob Ostrander.

Generous and gray-bearded, Ostrander is a fixture at brewfests and the sage historian of Indianabeer.com. He wrote a manuscript on the subject and was kind enough to talk at length over pints at Barley Island Brewing Company in Indianapolis.

A Quaker named Ezra Boswell was the first Hoosier brewer. Born in England, where he learned to brew, Boswell passed through North Carolina before settling in 1816 in Indiana Territory. Here, he opened a brewery, which he operated until his death in 1831.

By then breweries in the nation's nineteenth state had sprouted like corn as immigrants from Germany, France, England, Scotland, Ireland, Belgium, and Switzerland flocked to the fruited plain. The New Harmony Brewery was opened in 1818 by the Rappite Colony, religious utopians who considered beer an integral part of a perfect society. It closed in 1825, when another utopian, who felt just the opposite, bought the brewery in order to shut it down.

It foreshadowed things to come.

At first, Indiana's breweries were impinged only by the rule that they not sell any beer to Native Americans. Some played interesting bit roles in the American story. The Cephas Hawks brewery opened in Waterford in 1850 to attract settlers to buy nearby land. The Hoham/ Klinghammer brewery in Plymouth was used as a station on the Underground Railroad during the Civil War (and again as a speakeasy and bordello during Prohibition). The C. F. Schmidt Brewing Company was opened in 1858 by Peter Lieber, author Kurt Vonnegut's great-grandfather.

The breweries also cranked out massive amounts of beer. In 1889, the Terre Haute Brewing Company made 30,000 barrels. F. W. Cook made 75,000. Muessel Brewing Company made 100,000. For perspective,

3 Floyds, the largest contemporary brewery in Indiana, made 12,000 barrels in 2009.

In 1875, Indiana counted eighty-six breweries. Then came the fall.

Actually, the state had gone dry for six months in 1855, but the Indiana Supreme Court declared that law unconstitutional. Prohibitionists busybodied themselves at local levels and passed town laws banning taverns. Their efforts took a toll. By 1900, there were forty breweries in the state, less than half of what there were a generation earlier, though the ones that remained still produced massive amounts of beer. In 1915, there were thirty breweries. Then in 1918, when the state passed its second prohibition law, nineteen breweries fell. It was still a full two years before prohibition became a national law.

A few Indy breweries changed their name, slashed their staffs, and held on. Kammus in Mishawaka became Arrow Beverage. South Bend Brewing Association held on as South Bend Beverage and Ice. Centerville in Fort Wayne, which would emerge after Prohibition as Falstaff, became the Centlivre Ice and Cold Production Storage Company.

All of the breweries that remained open changed their product. Many churned out soda pop—grape soda, cream soda, blackberry soda, and root beer. Ostrander notes that many also made brisk sales of malt extract.

"You could just see a sign on the side that said, 'Do not add four gallons of water, do not boil for ninety minutes, do not add yeast,'" he said. "Of course people took matters into their own hands."

Wheedling brewers did too. Michael Schrick, who owned the Southern Indiana Ice and Beverage Company in New Albany (formerly the Paul Reising Brewing Company), tried to take advantage of a law that allowed beer to be brewed so long as it wasn't more than .05 percent alcohol.

"During prohibition, some places were making up to a 3 percent .05 percent beer," Ostrander said.

Schrick, whose beverage Hop-O was several percent alcohol, was arrested in 1922 for paying a prohibition agent $2,000 to look the other way. A newspaper report claimed that Schrick was planning to pay him $100,000. The Hop-O recipe would be recreated eighty-eight years later by the New Albanian Brewing Company in southern Indiana, giving contemporary consumers a taste of the past.

William J. Norton, of T. M. Norton Brewery in Anderson, also went to prison after federal agents arrested two of his truck drivers in 1923 for planning to drive to Cincinnati with a brew believed to be 5 percent alcohol.

In 1933, Gov. Paul McNutt cracked the state's "Bone-Dry" law and let 1,027 unlucky bastards out of prison.

Some brewers were just unlucky renaming their products. Zorn Brewery in Michigan City made the soft drink Zoro. Home Brewery in Indianapolis made a similar beverage called Homo.

A handful of breweries that survived Prohibition began brewing beer again. In the decades that followed, corporations bought and consolidated them. The G. Heileman Brewing Company bought remnants of Muessel Brewing Company and the Evansville Brewing Association and ratcheted up production to 1.3 million barrels a year by the time it shuttered in 1972. The Indiana Distilling Company, formerly Terre Haute Brewing Company, boasted the biggest bottling in the country after Prohibition, buoyed by the strength of their marquee brew, Champagne Velvet. But in 1958, an even bigger corporation bought them out and moved the factory to Chicago, where it closed in the 1980s.

In Indiana, as in the nation, behemoth brewing companies like Anheuser-Busch and Coors Brewing dominated local markets. Unable to touch their production, distribution, or advertising reach, the middle part of the twentieth century was a wasteland for the family brewery.

Mementos of the breweries that fell by the wayside still stand on the shelves in some of today's Hoosier breweries. Look closely in places like Lafayette Brewing Company, Broad Ripple Brewpub in Indianapolis, and Half Moon in Kokomo. You'll see cans, bottles, and crates from bygone breweries like F. W. Cook, the Indianapolis Brewing Company, Kamm & Schellinger, Lafayette Brewery Inc., Centlivre Brewing Company, Hoff-Brau, Great Crescent, The Indiana Brewing Association, Kiley Brewing Company, Guenther and Zwereck, Wabash Brewery, Hack & Simon, Walter-Raupfer, Rettig and Cole, and others.

By 1960, the four remaining family breweries in the state were all corporate owned. Drewery's, from Winnipeg, Canada, bought out the Muessel Brewery, founded by the Muessel family in South Bend in 1852. Centlivre Brewing Company, which began in 1862 in Fort Wayne, was sold to boat builders in Detroit who renamed the company Old Crown. The Terre Haute Brewing Company, which opened in 1837, eventually was sold to G. Heileman and then to a revamped Sterling. Berghoff Brothers, which opened in Fort Wayne in 1882, eventually became Falstaff. By 1980, only Heileman and Falstaff remained.

In 1987, the Indianapolis Brewing Company opened. It was the first new Hoosier brewery in thirty years. Though it lasted just a decade, it tapped the keg for things to come.

Just as the birth of Indiana brewing came courtesy of an Englishman, so too did its rebirth. John Hill, born in Middleborough, England, opened a brewpub in the Broad Ripple neighborhood of Indianapolis in 1990. He was inspired by a trip he took with his wife to a craft brewery in California. At the time, an archaic state law was still on the books that banned beer from being served under the same roof where it was brewed. Employees at the new Broad Ripple Brewpub were forced to keg their beer, wheel it out of the brewery through one door, and then back into the restaurant through a neighboring door. Hill, who in the eyes of the state owned two separate businesses, a brewery and a restaurant, proved he was crafty enough not only to make craft beer, but also to outfox an inane law.

When the state legalized brewpubs in 1993, it set the stage for a farmer's grip of brewpubs and breweries to open.

The new generation of family breweries, like 3 Floyds, Sun King, Power House, Shoreline, and Half Moon, to name just a few, showed innovation, originality, audaciousness, and enterprise; they were clearly built on the foundation laid by previous Hoosier brewers.

Some pay homage to that fact. The modern New Boswell Brewing Company in Richmond salutes Ezra Boswell, the state's first brewer. Maimed, Boswell wore a patch over an eye. So too does the pirate-looking gent on New Boswell's logo. New Albanian Brewery brewed a dark pilsner named Kaiser 2nd Reising in tribute to Paul Reising, who ran a brewery in the town for many years. People's Brewing, in Lafayette, chose their name not knowing it was once the name of a Terre Haute brewery a century earlier.

"When we found out about it," said People's Brewing co-owner and brewer Chris Johnson, "it was like being a part of continuing history."

Sometimes Indiana beer history repeats itself as comedy. The owner of the second Terre Haute Brewing Company tried to resurrect a 1901 recipe for a pre-Prohibition common ale, which a worker found while cleaning out the old warehouse. The newer brewer didn't quite get the recipe right.

"The beer wasn't that good," Ostrander said.

It didn't help that the new Terre Haute Brewing Company dubbed the swill Champagne Velvet, a name purchased from the Pabst Company. The original Champagne Velvet, brewed by the first Terre Haute Brewing Company, was popular throughout the Midwest. Those who remembered the classic didn't appreciate getting the New Coke treatment. In a case of history repeating itself, the second Terre Haute Brewing Company shut down too.

Some of the new generation of brewers went to great lengths to make history one of their brewing ingredients. Tom Coster, owner of Brickworks Brewery in Hobart, built his bar with antique bricks hauled up from the bottom of Amber Lake by his town's Aquatics Underwater Recovery and Rescue Unit.

"It was quite a unique experience," said diver Ronald Kurth, who remembers feeling around the mucky lake bottom for the remnants of Hobart's classic brickmaking factories.

Unfortunately Coster, like scores before him, learned that brewing in Indiana can be a perilous business venture. His brewery closed in 2010, having been open less than a year.

But around three dozen are succeeding, and more are coming. The most notable thing about this incredible resurrection of Indiana brewing is the quality of the beer, said Douglas A. Wissing, author of *One Pint at a Time: A Traveler's Guide to Indiana's Breweries.*

"It's important to recognize that Indiana is brewing world-class beer," he said. "We are disproportionately winning international and national awards."

As this second golden wave swells, more special beers are being brewed, more drinkers are delighting in their unique flavors, and more stories are being made. We tell those stories in this book, both for the casual craft beer fan, and for hardcore Hoosier historians like Ostrander, all of them anxious to taste Indiana brewing's next chapter.

Thanks, Bob. We owe you a pool of beer.

Brewpubs vs. Microbreweries

We'll be examining several different kinds of establishments in this book and it's important to know the difference between places. When many people think of breweries, they conjure up thoughts of large factories, billowing smokestacks, and thousands of clanking bottles heading down an automated line being filled, capped, labeled, and packaged. Companies like MillerCoors and Anheuser-Busch dominate the American beer landscape and have large breweries set up around the country to meet demand.

Indiana has no such facilities. Instead the Hoosier state is filled with smaller *microbreweries.* They typically produce fewer than six million barrels annually (a barrel contains about 31 gallons) and serve a smaller geographical area. These breweries bottle or can their beer and fill keg orders for bars and other customers.

A *brewpub* is essentially a restaurant that has brewing equipment. There are exceptions, but in most cases, their beer is available on the premises only and not in stores. However, customers can usually purchase *growlers*, half-gallon jugs to enjoy the beer at home.

The term *craft brewery* is also used a lot and can be interchangeable with brewpub and microbrewery. Simply put, the places mentioned in this book use quality ingredients, proper brewing methods, and embody a spirit reminiscent of earlier brewing pioneers.

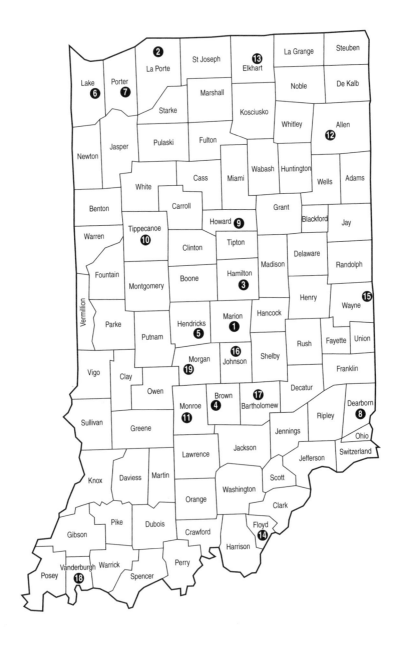

BREWERY LOCATIONS

book page

❶ Alcatraz Brewing Company 76

❷ Back Road Brewery 28

❸ Barley Island Brewing Company 51

❶ The Bier Brewery and Taproom 94

❹ Big Woods Brewing Company 53

❺ Black Swan Brewpub 61

❶ Broad Ripple Brewpub 82

❶ Brugge Brasserie 74

❻ Crown Brewing 18

❼ Figure Eight Brewing 26

❶ Flat12 Bierwerks 92

❽ Great Crescent Brewery 117

❾ Half Moon Restaurant & Brewery 48

❿ Lafayette Brewing Company 45

⓫ Lennie's/Bloomington Brewing Company 102

⓬ Mad Anthony Brewing Company 43

⓭ Mishawaka Brewing Company 24

⓮ The New Albanian Brewing Company 119

⓮ The New Albanian Brewing Company
Bank Street Brewhouse 121

⓯ New Boswell Brewing Company 57

⓰ Oaken Barrel Brewing Company 60

⓾ People's Brewing Company 40

⓱ Power House Brewing Company 114

❶ Ram Restaurant & Brewery 77

❶ Rock Bottom Restaurant & Brewery, College Park 86

❶ Rock Bottom Restaurant & Brewery, Downtown 84

❶ Scotty's Thr3e Wise Men Brewing Company 89

❷ Shoreline Brewery & Restaurant 30

❶ Sun King Brewery 80

❻ 3 Floyds Brewing Company 21

❺ Three Pints Brewing 63

❶ Triton Brewing Company 91

⓲ Turoni's Main Street Brewery 123

⓫ Upland Brewing Co. 104

❶ Upland Tasting Room 88

⓳ Wilbur BrewHause 55

name. Miller has recently indicated that he wants to move the operation closer to home, so it's possible that if he finds the right location, tours will be available at the new place.

Since we began research on this book, several other people have expressed interest or even filed papers with the intent of opening a brewery or brewpub. Most are in the Indianapolis area, meaning that soon there will be a wealth of local beer options for visitors and residents alike. We'll be keeping tabs on them via the website beerbriefing.com and will update as new breweries and brewpubs open.

It's also good to call in advance of a visit. Brewers take vacation just like the rest of us, and while there might be a sign on the door alerting the locals to the fact, we don't want you driving a long distance only to find they'll reopen next Monday.

As for tours, you'll see that many offer them by appointment or only on certain days. However, if you see employees poking around the brewery and ask nicely, they'll likely show you around. If you're lucky, they might even pour you a taste from the fermentation tanks.

Before You Hit The Road

It should go without saying, but please do not drink and drive. Know your limitations and if you decide that you're having too much fun and want to stay for a few more (and hey, who hasn't been there), just have the bartender call you a cab. We took turns driving while working on this trip and it helped not only with the writing, but gave us peace of mind knowing that we would be getting home safe each and every night.

While we crisscrossed the state in search of great beer, Nate, a musician, regularly played gigs at anyplace that would let him. In addition to his own songs, each set would include the Warren Zevon song "Lawyers, Guns, and Money." It became the de facto anthem of the writing process and roadtrip. Zevon, who passed away in 2003, was asked just before his death by David Letterman if he had learned anything now that he was facing his own mortality.

"Just how much you're supposed to enjoy every sandwich," Zevon replied.

In that spirit, as you take this book with you along your Hoosier state beer odyssey, we hope you'll take the occasion to enjoy every pint.

Cheers!

Chicagoland and the Great Lakes
Northern Indiana

Northern Indiana's character is shaped by two gargantuan entities that both offer opportunities for recreation, excitement, relaxation, and adventure. One is the city of Chicago and the other is Lake Michigan.

Our journey through this part of the state will give you breathtaking views of a great lake, a storied college town, and a landscape that is more geared to outdoor recreation than farming. In the winter months, visitors can experience what snow and cold in the Midwest are all about. But it's certainly better to visit in the warmer months.

Depending on where you are in this section, people will either refer to it as Illiana or Michiana, nods to the two states that share borders with the Hoosier State. Also important to know about this area is that the northwest corner of Indiana closest to Chicago operates on Central Time. Six counties—Lake, Porter, Newton, Jasper, La Porte, and Starke—operate one hour behind most of the state (there are counties in southern Indiana that are also on Central Time, and we'll address those in that chapter). This is important to note because if you're driving from, say the Mishawaka Brewing Company in Elkhart to the Back Road Brewery in La Porte, you could either be an hour late or an hour early for an appointment or tour if you're not aware of the change.

The most awesome natural feature in this region is the giant sand dunes that butt up to Lake Michigan. ***Indiana Dunes National Lakeshore*** and ***Indiana Dunes State Park*** preserve 15,000 acres of woods, marshes, bogs, rivers, dunes, and beaches. In the summertime, scores of vacationers flock here to swim, and in the winter hearty souls come for peace and solitude.

Trails that lead up the tallest dunes provide excellent views of the surrounding land, where industry met preservation behind a horizon of blue. Visitors can watch winds whip the most famous dune, Mount Baldy, like a scene out of *Lawrence of Arabia*, making it creep along at a rate of about 4 feet per year. Christine Livingston, spokeswoman for Indiana Dunes Tourism, called the area the top destination in the state.

"Once here, in addition to local breweries, you will find art galleries, theatre, museums, and great fine and casual dining within walking distance," she said. We couldn't agree more.

Lodging in the area: You can find a room for the night in just about any price range when visiting this part of the state. We found www.indianabedandbreakfast.org to be a great resource. Also check with the following convention and visitors bureaus, which often run specials with local hotels: South Bend/Mishawaka, www.exploresouthbend.org; Steuben County, www.lakes101.org; South Shore, www.southshorecva.com; City of Mishawaka, www.mishawakacity.com/visitors; Beyond the Beach Discovery Trail, www.beyondthebeachdiscoverytrail.org.

Area attractions: In South Bend is northwestern Indiana's largest attraction, the *University of Notre Dame* (www.nd.edu), home of the Fighting Irish. The school was founded in 1842 and is one of the nation's best-known colleges. It's also the location of the *College Football Hall of Fame* (www.collegefootball.org), at least for now—the Hall is planning to relocate to Atlanta in 2013. Those with a sweet tooth can tap their inner Willie Wonkas at the *South Bend Chocolate Company* (3300 West Sample Street, 574-233-2577, www.sbchocolate.com), housing one of the world's largest chocolate collections; visitors can see how the sweet stuff is made and indulge in samples. Classic-car lovers can check out the *Studebaker Museum* (201 South Chapin Street, 888-391-5600, www.studebakermuseum.org), where your every question about this classic American automobile will be answered. Golfers can tee up at the *Blackthorn Golf Club* (www.blackthorngolf.com) and the *Warren Golf Club* on the Notre Dame campus. River rats can raft and kayak the St. Joseph River on the East Race Waterway while rock climbers can enjoy the downtown park's new climbing wall (www.sbpark.org/parks/parks.htm).

Mishawaka has a famous Japanese garden called *Shiojiri Niwa* (1000 East Mishawaka Avenue, www.mishawakacity.com/shiojiriniwa). Inspired by its counterpart in Shiojiri, Japan, the garden will transport you to the Far East.

Chesterton is home to the wildlife oasis *Coffee Creek Park* (www.coffeecreekwc.org). The *Westchester Township History Museum* (700 West Porter Avenue, Chesterton, 219-983-9715, http://wpl.lib.in.us/

museum) showcases local artwork plus displays on the area's first environmentalists.

In Porter, visitors can learn about the region's earliest European settlers, who opened fur-trading posts in 1822 at *Bailly Homestead* and *Chellberg Farm*, two historic sites that sit side-by-side in the national lakeshore (www.nps.gov/indu/index.htm).

In the nearby Moraine section of the Dunes region, visitors can take a break from beer at *Anderson's Vineyard and Winery* (430 East U.S. 6, Valparaiso, 219-464-4936, www.andersonwinery.com).

See the nation's first red meat, buffalo, on the hoof at the *Broken Wagon Bison Farm* (563 West 450 North Road, Hobart, 219-759-3523). Try your luck for salmon and trout in nearby Salt Creek at the *Chustak Public Fishing Area* (www.dnr.in.gov).

Goshen is home to *The Old Bag Factory* (1100 North Chicago Avenue, www.oldbagfactory.com), where shoppers can get artisan crafts ranging from pottery to quilts.

In North Judson, check out *Dunns Bridge County Park* (www.njwt .lib.in.us/articles3.htm). Its namesake bridge, according to legend, was constructed with scrap metal from the world's first Ferris wheel, which had been built for the World's Columbian Exposition in Chicago in 1893.

Kankakee has plenty of natural and cultural significance, including its setting as the spot where the train "pulled out" in the Steve Goodman–penned song "City of New Orleans," made famous by Arlo Guthrie.

Other beer sites: *Mad Anthony Brewing Company Lake City Tap House* (113 East Center Street, Warsaw, www.madbrew.com) is one of three satellite locations that serve beer from the Fort Wayne brewery, but do not have actual brewing equipment on premises. The other two are *Mad Anthony's Old State Alehouse* (526 South Main Street, Elkhart, 574-293-5100) and *Mad Anthony Tap Room* (114 North Main Street, Auburn, 260-927-0500).

Although it's a chain, *Buffalo Wild Wings* (23 Pine Lake Avenue, La Porte, 219-324-9464, www.buffalowildwings.com) has a decent tap selection, including offerings from the Back Road Brewery.

In Michigan City, our pals at the Shoreline Brewery recommend *McGinnis Pub* (227 West 7th Street, 219-872-8200, www.mcginnispub .com) and *Matey's Restaurant* (110 Franklin Street, 219-872-9471, www .mateysrestaurant.com).

The Pub (408 W. Cleveland Road, Mishawaka) serves beers from the Mishawaka Brewing Company, but the suds are produced at their production brewery in Elkhart.

You don't go to the *Linebacker Lounge* (1631 South Bend Avenue, South Bend, 574- 289-0186, www.backer-nd.com) for the craft beer; you go for the sense of tradition, the thoroughly college-like experience, and a chance to see some Fighting Irish. Hoosier beer is plentiful at **Bone Dry Bar & Grill** (3805 Ridge Road, Highland, 219-838-2442), a place where the Chicago Cubs are idolized, burgers are satisfying, and both the music and company are good.

Beer Geeks Pub (3030 45th Street, Highland, 219-513-9795, beergeeks pub.com) With twenty rotating craft taps and cask ales, this relatively new bar celebrates the downright nerdy side of craft beer. Murals on the walls depict famous smarty-pants holding beers. Everyone from Doc Brown of *Back to the Future* fame to Yoda and Albert Einstein are enjoying a pint of well-made beer. You should stop in and join them.

Crown Brewing

211 South East Street, Crown Point, IN 46307
(219) 663-4545 • www.crownbrewing.com

The portal on the side of the Lake County Jail busted open on March 3, 1934. Out walked famous gangster John Dillinger.

Brandishing a hand-carved wooden pistol dyed black with shoe polish, according to a now legendary newspaper report, Dillinger had locked up the prison employees and raided their arsenal, picking up two real, loaded submachine guns. With accused murderer Herbert Youngblood in tow, Dillinger descended a small staircase into an alleyway between the four-story, red-brick prison and a neighboring boiler room, where Sheriff Lillian Holley had parked her new V8 Ford.

Dillinger broke into the garage and stole the top cop's ride, having yanked the ignition wires out of two other cars. Dillinger took two hostages, a fingerprint technician and the prison mechanic, and made them drive him across the plains, away from that Alcatraz in the corn—the one policemen said he would never escape.

"It's a pretty cool story," says Crown Brewing co-owner Dave Bryan, standing in Dillinger's path, explaining the getaway.

Today Crown Brewing calls that boiler room next to the now-defunct prison its kitchen, which appropriately serves a Jailbreak Burger. Along with partner Tim Walsh, Bryan opened the brewery in June 2008. Today there are between six and nine microbrews on tap, including the brewery's flagship Special Forces IPA, named in honor of a local soldier who helped catch Barzan Ibrahim al-Tikriti, Saddam Hussein's half-brother. (That soldier's identity has never been revealed, but brewery employees say he has visited and enjoyed the beer named in his honor.) The bar is made of polished, dark calico marble, and atop, next to the taps, sits a glass jar filled with hops. Adorning the walls is a Dillinger wanted poster and a framed newspaper photo of three men standing with tommy guns beside the jail under the headline, "Jail That Could Not Hold Killer."

Above the bar hangs one of the coolest chandeliers in any Indiana brewery; it's made of a metal sheet the size of a small pickup bed, with more than a hundred brown beer bottles lit with white holiday lights. The artwork was commissioned by local electrician and friend of the brewery Tom Frame. The bottles on the chandelier once sported Miller Lite labels, prompting Chris Stanek, director of sales and marketing, to joke, "Finally, a use for Miller Lite."

Brewmaster Steve Mazylewski, who had worked professionally across Illinois and in Arkansas, is friendly with other regional brewers, including Nick Floyd at 3 Floyd's in Munster and Sam Strupek, who owns Shoreline Brewery. Through the latter he heard about the job opening in Crown Point.

Mazylewski's first move was to increase production. Today Crown Point is available in bottles and is served on tap at a few area restaurants and bars. Realizing that many customers came for pizzas cooked in the restaurant, Mazylewski also brewed lighter beers that could be enjoyed with pies.

"I brought lagers to the brewery because I'm a huge lager brewer," he said. "We have beers geared toward beer lovers, but 80 percent of our clientele is going to come in and just want some beer with their pizza." Crown also crafts a delicious root beer.

A Friday afternoon visit shows that the brewery does a brisk business in growlers. Many locals stop by regularly for their half-gallon refills.

The Pick: Marzenfest is a hearty beer to enjoy in springtime, when you're shaking the last of the snow off your boots and looking forward to warmer weather. This robust brew is like another of its German counterparts, the Oktoberfest Lager, but it's served in the opposite season.

Beers brewed: Special Forces IPA, Industrial Porter, PATRICK, Witbier, Crown Light, Weizenheimer Weiss, Jailhouse Bock, Winter Warlock, Blueberry Light, Belgian Dubbel, Marzenfest, Crown Brown, Blueberry Wheat, Celtic Pride Stout, Kill'em Ale, CB Root Beer, Celtic Coffee Stout

"The taste of the beer is great," said Paul MacDonald, a pipe fitter from nearby Hebron, as he walked out with a growler of Special Forces IPA. "Every one I've ever had here is excellent."

The town of Crown Point is steeped in brewing history. In 1895, three investors from Chicago opened Crown Brewing Company on West Goldsborough Street. The brewery supplied area taverns with suds, which sold for a nickel and generally came with a free lunch, according to Crown Point historians. For years the brewery dumped its waste into a ditch in Crown Point, which polluted nearby farmers' fields. Today, all that remains of that operation is a garage that stores livestock-hauling trucks.

In 1910, the original Crown Brewing Company was forced to move to West Hammond, which is now Calumet City. After its move and a name change to Great Lakes Brewing, Prohibition dealt the business its final death knell.

Still, it is Dillinger's specter that looms larger over today's Crown Brewing than any other figure in history. As the brewery was undergoing its finishing touches in March and April of 2008, the Dillinger biopic *Public Enemies*, starring Johnny Depp, was being filmed at the old jail next door.

Co-owner Bryan said the first dollar that his business made came courtesy of Hollywood. Next to the bar sits the base of an 80-foot brick chimney once used by the jail's boiler room. Bryan had the old structure refurbished and now hangs a sign on it that reads, "Crown." On the day he hired a crane operator to run to the top of the chimney and put fresh cement between the old bricks, *Public Enemies* director Michael Mann paid a visit.

"He said that they were shooting a scene with the jail in the background and the crane was in the shot," Bryan said. "I explained to him that it was costing me money for the crane and Mann said, 'Just bill me.' A week later, a check came in the mail."

Stories of the temporary Hollywood takeover of Crown Point are nearly as abundant as old gangster tales. Jeff Bles, a town resident who works for Pepsi, said that his wife Peggy waited with a throng of fans for a picture of Johnny Depp.

"It was an exciting time," he said. "I just come to pick up pizza and have the blonde lager."

Crown Brewing

Opened: June 2008
Owners: Tim Walsh, Dave Bryan

Brewer: Steve Mazylewski

System: 7-barrel Bavarian Brewing Technologies, with 4 fermenters and 6 serving tanks.

Production: 500 barrels estimated for 2010

Brewpub hours: Monday through Thursday, 11 A.M. to 11 P.M.; Friday and Saturday, 11 A.M. to midnight; Sunday, 3 P.M. to 11 P.M.

Tours: Sundays at 4 P.M. or by appointment.

Take-out beer: Kegs, growlers, and 22-ounce bottles of Special Forces IPA and Crown Brown.

Food: American cuisine, specializing in pizza.

Extras: Half-price pints on Thursday. $8 growler refills on Friday.

Special considerations: Handicapped-accessible

Parking: Free lot, plus street parking.

3 Floyds Brewing Company

9750 Indiana Parkway, Munster, IN 46321
(219) 922-3565 • www.3floyds.com

If breweries were crayons, 3 Floyds would be a 64-pack of Crayolas. One wall is yellow, the other is teal, another is blue, and yet another is purple. Hanging on those walls are big, colorful paintings of logos for brews named Rabbid Rabbit, Behemoth, and the notorious Gumball Head. None would appear out of place in *Mad* magazine.

"It's not normal," said owner Nick Floyd. "That's our motto."

3 Floyds had been a successful production brewery for more than a decade before anyone worried about interior design. The first brewing facility was in Hammond, Nick said, "because 5,000 square feet was $500 bucks a month back then." The operation moved to Munster in 2000.

The company made its first baby steps toward becoming what it is today when it started selling beer outside in a 20-square-foot area from a kiosk featuring industrial chairs and a roll-up counter. There, patrons could buy growlers to go. Considering their ever-growing popularity, the three Floyds—father Mike and his sons Simon and Nick—devised a business plan to open their brewpub. For $1,000, a patron could buy stock in the business and get a free pint a day. More than one hundred signed on for varying amounts of money, and thus the company had the capital to become a full-fledged brewpub in 2006.

Tap handles from hundreds of microbrews encircle the tops of the walls at 3 Floyds. There is also a bevy of toys and collectors' items decorating shelves, including *Simpsons* memorabilia and figurines of Chuck D, Flavor Flav, the Ramones, the Notorious B.I.G., Pee-wee Herman and Ozzy Osbourne. At one spot a Cheech and Chong lunchbox holds a *Texas Chainsaw Massacre* doll.

The menu features such delicious items as pizza and soft, savory mussels. Silverware and condiments are provided in the same cardboard six-pack holders that serve bottled 3 Floyds beers. There is one flat-screen TV near the bar; it hangs under a scarf for the English soccer team Arsenal, and during a visit it was broadcasting a game. A kung-fu movie was projected on the only white wall in the building.

The bar area features several low-lying couches, and on each table in the dining area was a small glass vase containing a real, red rose.

Fred Kuzel, a grant writer who lives in Chicago, discovered 3 Floyds by Googling microbreweries. Since his discovery in 2009 he said he makes the forty-minute drive across the state line two times each month.

"Everything I've had here has been really good foodwise and beerwise," he said. "And they change beers a lot."

Nick Floyd said that the brewery produces around fifty different styles of beer.

A window in the back of the dining room looks into the gigantic brewing area in a warehouse behind the brewpub. Nick learned brewing at Chicago's Siebel Institute. "I was twenty-one then, and I've been brewing professionally ever since," he said. "In 1996 I got tired of working for other people and decided to open 3 Floyds with my dad and brother." Despite the recent tough economy, Nick said the brewery's production grew 40 percent in 2009.

In addition to house-brewed beers, half the taps at 3 Floyds pour guest beers, typically the best in the region. Their names are written in colored chalk on a blackboard that hangs to the right of the bar. The board is as crazy-colorful as the wackiest of 3 Floyd's logos. Brewer Andrew Maston said that artwork and beer at 3 Floyd's have a chicken-and-egg relationship.

The Pick: The easy choice would be the annual Dark Lord, an Imperial Russian stout, but the recipe varies from year to year, and while they all are good, you're better off with one of the brewery's year-round offerings. We like Gumball Head for the way it redefined—for the better—the American wheat beer style. The big guys on the playing field have tried to get into this market, but their product doesn't even come close to the brew produced by the Floyd family.

Beers brewed: Year-round: Alpha King, Robert the Bruce, Pride & Joy, Gumball Head, Dreadnaught. Seasonals: Behemoth, Dark Lord, Rabbid Rabbit.

"We have art that's inspired by our beer and we have beer that's inspired by our art," he said. A testament to the nexus of art, beer-loving, and fanaticism that converge at 3 Floyds are photos on the wall of body parts tattooed with brilliant 3 Floyds logos.

The brewery is renowned for its annual Dark Lord Day, the last Saturday in April, when the team taps kegs of an enormous Russian Imperial stout that is 15 percent alcohol and hits with an equally huge flavor.

Behind the bar hangs a framed picture of Lemmy from the seminal punk-metal band Motörhead that reads, "You don't have to be Motörhead to enjoy good beer." A shelf above the bar holds rows of growlers, and underneath, goblet-shaped beer glasses hang like bats. The different shapes and sizes are testament to the diversity of the brews at 3 Floyds and the company's commitment to ensuring tipplers have a top-notch tasting experience.

3 Floyds Brewing Company

Opened: 1996; brewpub, 2006

Owners: Nick Floyd, Michael Floyd, Simon Floyd

Brewers: Nick Floyd, Chris Boggess, Barnaby Struve, Andrew Mason

System: 35-barrel system from China, with 14 fermenters.

Production: 12,000 barrels in 2009; 17,000 barrels estimated for 2010.

Brewpub hours: Monday through Friday, 11:30 A.M. to midnight; Saturday, noon to midnight; Sunday, noon to 10 P.M.

Tours: Saturdays at 3 P.M.

Take-out beer: Growlers of all year-round beers, bottles.

Food: American and French cuisine

Extras: Movie screenings

Special considerations: Handicapped-accessible

Parking: Free lot

Mishawaka Brewing Company

2414 Lowell Street, Elkhart, IN 46516
(574) 295-5348

Even with the correct address, some breweries are easier to find than others. A case in point is Mishawaka Brewing Company, located in Elkhart. Seasoned brewery travelers have seen their fair share of old factories in, shall we call them, less desirable neighborhoods; they can spot the tell-tale signs, like a grain silo, or simply follow their noses if it's a brew day.

Mishawaka Brewing, however, threw us for a loop. "This can't be right," we muttered as we drove up and down the mostly residential Lowell Street, off Elkhart's main drag. Finally, on the third pass we noticed a small brewery logo sticker in the rear window of a silver Ford van parked in a driveway.

Tom Schmidt, owner and brewer, greeted us warmly in the tiny space that serves as an office on the other side of the front door and proceeded to give us the nickel tour. His son, Rick, who is also a brewer, was set up on a collapsible canvas camp chair alongside the brewkettles. He was guzzling coffee from an extra large takeaway cup and would occasionally pipe in as his father told the story of Mishawaka.

They started as a brewpub in 1992 in the actual city of Mishawaka, a short drive from South Bend and the campus of Notre Dame. Riding high on the brewpub boom of the early 1990s, the family had good business and soon started selling 22-ounce bottles of their beer, which they still do to this day.

The brewing space was tiny, and Tom said they produced about 1,100 to 1,300 barrels a year. Adding to their popularity was the advent of Four Horsemen Irish-style red ale, the label emblazoned with an iconic photo of four Notre Dame football players from 1924. "People loved it," said Rick from the back of the room.

Eventually, Tom got the idea that he wanted to build a smaller production brewery, something that could handle a larger volume of beer and

The Pick: Call it a cliché, but one can't help but get into the spirit of Notre Dame and its proud football tradition when sipping on a Four Horsemen Irish Ale. At 5.6 percent ABV, it has a nice malt character and just the slightest hops bite. Glass isn't allowed inside Notre Dame Stadium, but that shouldn't prevent you from bringing it for the great American practice of tailgating.

Beers brewed: Seven Mules Kick Ass Ale, Jibber Jabber Java Stout, Indiana Pale Ale, Four Horsemen Irish Ale.

even serve as a nice refuge from the restaurant itself. He got his chance in 2004 when he was able to buy a full fifteen-barrel system from a now defunct Michigan brewery.

"I didn't know what I was going to do with it, but it was too good a deal to pass up," he said. So he stored the equipment at a warehouse another son owned. Eventually, in 2005 a building across the street on Lowell Street became available, and Schmidt saw his chance to start his production brewery.

"Took at least a year to get everything started," chimed in Rick, who was then brewing at the restaurant. "I'm most proud that we installed it all ourselves," said the father.

It's been said that farmers make wine and scientists make beer. Tom was a scientist long before he brewed his first batch. A food scientist for Myles Laboratories to be exact. In 1986, he attended a craft brewer conference in Oregon and promptly filled two notebooks with as much information as he could obtain. He returned home and began home brewing, "experimenting until I got it right."

In 2008, the family closed the brewpub, citing declining sales. Tom still gets calls and emails from former patrons, however, asking for certain recipes. The Schmidts continue to operate a drinking establishment called The Pub at 408 W. Cleveland Road in Mishawaka. They don't brew on premises, but the full line of Mishawaka brews is available on draft or in bottles.

Aside from Four Horsemen, Mishawaka makes a full line of beers that includes seasonal and regular offerings like a pale ale and java stout. Tom quit drinking a few years back, although he still tastes the beer "for quality control" and then spits it out.

As we finished the interview, the son called from the back of the brewery. It was time for the father to stop talking and help Rick clean out the mash tun.

Mishawaka Brewing Company

Opened: 2006
Owner: Tom Schmidt
Brewer: Tom Schmidt, Rick Schmidt
System: 15-barrel Specific Mechanical
Production: 700 barrels in 2009. 700 barrels estimated for 2010.
Tours: By appointment
Take-out beer: Bottles, kegs
Special considerations: Handicapped-accessible
Parking: In the driveway in front

Figure Eight Brewing

1555 West Lincolnway #105, Valparaiso, IN 46385
(219) 477-2000 • www.figure8brewing.com

The figure eight knot that connects a rope to a rock climber's safety harness can be the only thing separating that climber from a free fall.

There is a parallel between that knot and Figure Eight Brewing, one of Indiana's newest places to tie one on. The brewery opened in March 2010, the brain child of rock-climbing enthusiast Tom Uban.

"That knot is very essential," he said. "Your life is relying on that knot structure."

A software consultant by trade, Uban said he reached middle age and began to think about things he'd like to do more in the second act of his life. He wanted to knot his work to his passion.

"I was looking for something new and exciting to keep me busy," he said. "Something a little more hands-on that could challenge me."

The idea came to him after he visited nearby Back Road Brewery to pick up a keg to share with some of his rock-climbing buddies.

"I thought, 'It could be fun to do something like this,'" he said. "Most of my friends like good craft beers over high-volume, low-taste beer."

A Valparaiso native, Uban said he settled on his location because it is only minutes from his house. Figure Eight is based in a small warehouse. Inside there is equipment for brewing, equipment for farming that Uban converted into brewing gear, and devices Uban built himself. Near the brewing tanks is a tank originally used for dairy farming that Uban turned into a mash tun, where grains are malted. On the second floor, Uban built a roller mill to crack open, but not crush, his grains.

Tom's eighty-one-year-old father, Earl Uban, helped in the construction of the brewery. He built the wooden tables in the L-shaped merchandise room, which seats fourteen.

"Whatever he needed I was happy to help," Earl Uban said, paying his son a visit before the brewery's grand opening.

The Pick: An emerging trend among brewers is to use rye in their beers. Figure Eight does not disappoint with its Rye Knot. It clocks in at 7.2 percent ABV and is a cross between a strong stout and even stronger porter. Nice woodsy aromas make this beer a must-try.

Beers brewed: First Ascent, Ro Shampo, Camp 4 Brown Ale, Rye Knot, Offwidth, Where Lizards Dare, Twist of F8, Snake Pro IPA.

Figure Eight promises to be the only brewery in the state, perhaps the nation, with an indoor climbing wall. Uban said he plans to turn a 16-foot wall into a rock climbers' practice space. Wait for hilarious scenes when Uban's passion for climbing meets up with his beer.

Figure Eight features a handful of brews that Uban developed while homebrewing, a hobby he began in the mid-1980s. The brews include a Belgian honey lager appropriately named First Ascent, a hoppy tipple called Rye Knot, an ale similar to Newcastle Brown, and an Imperial red ale named Ro Shampo after one of his favorite places to rock climb in Kentucky's Red River Gorge.

The artwork for each beer's logo comes from a connection Uban made during one of his last big computer jobs. From 1993 through 1999, Uban wrote the software for pinball games for Williams/Bally company, one of the nation's last large-scale manufacturers of pinball games. Through that job he met artist Greg Freres, whose work adorns many pinball machines.

"My artist is one of the really good pinball artists from those days," Uban said.

Freres's work is both vivid and whimsical. The label he made for Uban's maiden brew, First Ascent, depicts a woman climber about to reach a rocky summit where a giant bear sits, smiling and licking his chops.

Uban distributes his beers to liquor stores and taverns in northwest Indiana. He sells growlers and will soon begin bottling 22-ouncers. In keeping with the trend of brewers sporting distinctive facial hair, Uban has a pronounced soul patch. He said he chose a motto for his brewery based on his decision to pursue his ambition. The motto is "Harness Your F8."

"I am passionate about certain things," he said. "And I am harnessing them."

Figure Eight Brewing

Opened: March 2010
Owner: Tom Uban
Brewer: Tom Uban
System: 7-barrel single infusion mash
Production: 350 barrels estimated for 2010
Brewpub hours: Thursday and Friday, 5 P.M. to 8 P.M.; Saturday and Sunday, 1 P.M. to 5 P.M.
Take-out beers: Growlers, 22-ounce bottles
Special considerations: Handicapped-accessible
Parking: Free lot

Back Road Brewery

308 Perry Street, La Porte, IN 46350
(219) 362-7623 • www.backroadbrewery.com

Back Road Brewery is appropriately named. It is located a few blocks from the revitalized Main Street in La Porte, inside a historic warehouse that rests hard against train tracks on a back road. There, Chuck Krcilek is living out his dream.

In the late 1980s and early '90s, he was flying by day and homebrewing at night. A Purdue University graduate, he completed the professional pilot program and had begun working as a flight instructor.

After a few years, the entrepreneurial itch struck. Krcilek realized that the brewing landscape was pretty bleak, with just Goose Island in Chicago and Mishawaka Brewing to the east serving as local breweries. He borrowed money and put a second mortgage on his house to open the Brick Road Brewing Company in August 1996.

La Porte was once known for its brick-paved streets, and Krcilek had also laid a 10-by-100-foot brick driveway by hand at his house. Even their old building had a brick parking lot. So Brick Road became the name. Simple. Easy to remember. Nice backstory.

In the first nine months, everything was going well despite operating on a shoestring budget. Then Krcilek got a letter from the Brick Brewing Company in Ontario, Canada, telling him they owned the rights to the name and that he must change his brewery's name or face a lawsuit.

"I wasn't going to give them any money," recalled Krcilek while sitting at a beat-up table in the front room of the 2,500-square-foot brewery. "So, I replaced the "r" and "i" with an a."

Brick Road Brewing became Back Road Brewing. The Brick Layers Ale became Back Road Ale. His corporate structure stayed the same.

The Pick: We don't often go for fruit-flavored beers. But the Blueberry Ale was refreshing—even in the dead of winter when we visited. Krcilek does a tester batch each February, an early taste of spring, to give people hope that a thaw is close at hand. It was snowing outside and temps were in the 20s, but a sip of the effervescent brew made me hopeful. Not too sweet, not too tart, slight malt finish.

Beers brewed: Back Road Ale, Belle Gunness Stout, American Pale Ale, Midwest IPA, Millennium Lager, Maple City Gold, No. Nine Barleywine-Style Ale, Blueberry Ale, Belgian-Style Wit, Aviator Dopplebock, Christmas Ale, Autumn Ale.

"They were cool with it," Krcilek said of his northern counterparts. "From there, things just took off."

Everywhere, it seemed, except La Porte. Early on, Krcilek was busy brewing and then driving bottles to cities that were willing to sell his beer—Lafayette at two hours away, Indianapolis at three hours away, and Bloomington at four hours and fifteen minutes away.

Meanwhile in his hometown, locals would stop by, scratch their heads, and ask when he was going to brew a beer like Coors Light. They would ask what beer had the most mild flavor. But he hung in there and created an IPA recipe that made people stand up and take notice. The locals began coming around more and more, and area restaurants started carrying his beers on tap.

Back Road still brews less than six hundred barrels a year, making it one of the smallest breweries in the state, but that doesn't mean it's not ambitious. Krcilek has created about sixty different recipes, and most were one-time offerings.

There are staples, however, like the Belle Gunness Stout, named after a female serial killer who lived and did other nefarious things in La Porte in the early 1900s. At 5 percent ABV, the Back Road Ale, a dry-hopped session beer with a nice, malty aroma, remains the best-selling offering and a source of local pride.

Krcilek, taking a few minutes to chat between making deliveries, said he likes the size of his brewery and has no plans to become a major player, something many breweries are too focused on.

He repeats the same phrase several times during our chat: Big brewery, big headaches. Small brewery, small headaches.

It boils down to this, he says: "Do your local folks support you? That's a better measure of how good you are."

They don't advertise, have a modest website, and have reigned in their distribution to just the La Porte area, although Back Road beer does make it to Indy and points south now and again. Still, people come to the pale yellow-painted building from far and wide for a tour each Saturday.

There's not too much to the place itself. A few taps in the wall against the walk-in refrigerator and brewing equipment cramped in the back, sectioned off by heavy clear-plastic strips, the same you see in meat lockers.

The walls are covered in beer labels and coasters, weaving a sort of brewery tapestry. It started with Krcilek's own collection and was quickly added to by visitors and friends, many of whom have mailed Krcilek new items from around the globe. When we visited there was a large stack piled in the back patiently waiting to be added to the mosaic. With wall space at a premium, the ceiling would likely be next.

Among the coasters and labels is a wooden propeller hanging from the rafters. It's from a post–World War II Aeronca Champion, the same one Krcilek used to fly. Some of his Indiana Brewer's Guild awards hang from each side.

Although it's been years since he's operated a plane, Krcilek is still flying high with his brewery.

Back Road Brewery

Opened: 1996
Owners: Chuck Krcilek, Jim Hannon
Brewers: Chuck Krcilek, Jim Hannon
System: CDC and used equipment
Production: 600 barrels
Tours: Saturday from 1 P.M. to 4 P.M. No appointment necessary.
Take-out beers: Bottles, growlers, 2.5-gallon Party Pigs.
Special considerations: Handicapped-accessible
Parking: Free

Shoreline Brewery & Restaurant

208 Wabash Street, Michigan City, IN 46360
(219) 879-4677 • www.shorelinebrewery.com

Shoreline Brewery sits alarmingly close to a giant cooling tower for a coal-fired power plant that looks conspicuously like the nuclear power plant that employs Homer Simpson in the fictional Springfield.

"It's a coal plant, but everybody thinks it's a nuclear tower there," said owner and brewer Sam Strupeck. "We poke fun at the non-locals, and even the locals, who think it's a nuclear tower." The brewery's top-selling T-shirt depicts a Matt Groening-esque three-eyed cartoon fish and reads, "Don't Drink the Water, Drink The Beer."

The beers themselves, supercharged with hops and often packing a hefty alcohol slug, are no laughing matter. "I'm a hop-head," boasts Strupeck. "The hop flower is very interesting to me; some are peppery, some are citrusy, they're kind of the spice of beer."

The Pick: Don't Panic English Pale Ale: Mostly Harmless.

Beers brewed: Ly-Co-Ki-We Kölsch, Stella Blue, Don't Panic English Pale Ale, Queen Mum India Pale Ale, Benny's American Pale Ale, Three Sum IIPA, Beltaine Scottish Ale, Singing Sands Oatmeal Stout.

Strupeck opened Shoreline in August 2005. Prior to that he worked as a brewer at the now-defunct Aberdeen Brewing Company in nearby Valparaiso, honing skills he first developed as a homebrewer in college. When Aberdeen shuttered, Strupeck thought about starting a restaurant in Chicago. Then he changed his mind.

He opted instead to set up shop in an abandoned building that once housed a golf-ball factory, next to the power tower in Michigan City. From his time at Aberdeen he knew that a microbrewery in the region could draw a good crowd in the winter and figured that he could draw better than Aberdeen in the summer because of Shoreline's proximity to Lake Michigan.

"I wanted an old building close to the lakefront," Strupeck said. "This was one of the only places in Indiana to find that."

He and business partners set about building Shoreline's rustic, knotty pine and brick interior, occasionally finding stray golf balls during renovations. Strupeck built a stage to showcase local musicians who perform original compositions, as well as national touring acts. He never charges a cover.

"So many of the bars around here just want cover bands," he said. "I figure if people come to drink something different, they might want to hear something original too."

Prior to its days as a golf-ball factory, legend has it that the building was used by the Alaskan Lumber Company, a printing press, and the neighboring Northern Indiana Public Service Company, which used it as a carriage house.

A wall that used to be a garage door is papered with posters from all the bands that play Shoreline, adding a nifty visual variation to the wood surroundings. Three-pronged, wooden ceiling fans whir overhead. To the left of the poster-covered door is a giant blackboard on which the names of brews on tap, as well as beers that are coming soon, are written in bright, colorful chalk. A smattering of local art hangs on the walls also.

Perhaps the most unique visual stimulus in the brewery are the mug-club steins, possibly the most unique in the state. Each one is an original work of art by Devin Somerville, a glassblower who lives in Wisconsin. The mugs are awash in swirls of color not dissimilar to designs found on bongs in head shops. The mugs all sit behind the bar, a perfect spot for tasters to contemplate their spectacle.

Joining the mug club requires a first-time fee of $140, but the bulk of that goes for the mug itself, an original work of art that the member is welcome to take home even if his or her membership lapses. Because of the limited space for the mugs, there can only ever be 210 mug club members at a time. As of February 2010, there were no plastic cups holding the space of a swirly, glass mug. That's the Shoreline signal that the mug club has a vacancy.

Bob Beckner owns one of the mugs, and enjoys filling it with Shoreline's Foggy Loggy. "There are different flavors here," he said. "I enjoy them over regular-brand beers."

Shoreline's strongest beers are aged in bourbon barrels and sealed with wax in old wine bottles. Strupeck said Shoreline's strong ales and Imperial stouts all get the bourbon-barrel treatment.

As this is Cubs country, a few Wrigley Field mementos hang to the right of the bar. Above the double doors leading to an outside patio that seats about thirty-five hangs a sign that reads, "The Friendly Confines," Wrigley Field's nickname. This spot is also where Shoreline holds its annual chili cook-off, Strupeck said.

On a shelf high above the bar, above the large picture windows looking in on the brewing tanks, sit pint glasses and growlers from breweries around the country. Underneath them sit some decorative cans of Drewrey's beer, brewed in South Bend, as well as Shoreline gift baskets that include a growler and two pint glasses. Blues music wafts over the stereo.

There are funny T-shirts and souvenir Frisbees on display just above the bar. Shoreline's sense of humor isn't limited to its tasting room. Above the urinals in the men's room hangs a framed classic black-and-white photograph of labor union members marching in Newark, New Jersey, in 1931 carrying signs that read, "We Want Beer."

The flavors in Shoreline's food really pop. Their grilled shrimp wrap with savory rice, one of Strupeck's specialty dishes, is delicious. Shoreline pairs its menu with its beers, resulting in some excellent matches, such as Sum Nug India Pale Ale with a Cajun shrimp wrap or Lost Sailor Imperial Stout with filet mignon.

Interestingly, Strupeck turned vegetarian in 1994 after working at a butcher shop. Though his menu doesn't reflect his dietary choice, his beers do. "As far as brewing goes, generally it is a vegetarian process," he said. "Our beer is definitely vegan on top of it."

Shoreline also brews barley wine, and in the summer of 2010 started bottling its Beltaine and Sum Nug brews in 22-ounce bottles. That fall it was set to start bottling in 12-ounce bottles also. "We're gradually growing, the next step for us is moving into some production but in a smaller scale; we're not looking to grow real fast," Strupeck said.

He said he wants to make sure the quality of his beers, not the scope of his ambition, drive Shoreline's growth. "I think a lot of places seem to have grown a little too fast and the quality of the beer is maybe compromised a little," he said. "Slow and steady is fine with me."

Shoreline Brewery & Restaurant

Opened: 2005

Owner: Sam Strupeck

Brewer: Sam Strupeck

System: 10-barrel brewing system with nine fermentation tanks and one bright tank.

Production: 1,500 barrels in 2009; 1,500 estimated for 2010.

Take-out beer: Growlers

Tours: By appointment

Brewpub hours: Sunday through Thursday, 11 A.M. to 11 P.M.; Friday and Saturday, 11 A.M. to 2 A.M.; kitchen open until 10 P.M. daily.

Food: American bistro style

Extras: Live bands on Saturdays, open mic on Tuesdays, $2 Brewer's Selection pints on Wednesdays.

Special consideration: Handicapped-accessible

Parking: Free lot, street parking

Beer Travel

Upon hearing that we were writing a book about beer, a lot of friends gave us high fives. Other people smirked when they talked about the "research" that we would have to conduct.

The reality, however, is that traveling from brewery to brewery is more than just drinking. It's a whole experience of discovering a new town, state, or country. For us, it's a privilege when people share their stories and we're able to make new friends with likeminded people at the bar.

Traveling to a brewery rather than your local store for a six-pack can open new doors. It gives you a chance to try a beer on draft or sample brews that don't have a distribution network. You can see first-hand the work that goes into making beer. At brewpubs, there are new foods to try and local stories to hear. As the American craft beer movement grows, so does the desire of drinkers to learn even more and to pry into the process behind their favorite suds. Breweries, it seems, are happy to oblige, offering experiences that go well beyond popping the top on a bottle.

Brewery tours are not new, of course. Back in the late 1800s, Anheuser-Busch recognized that consumers were interested in a behind-the-scenes look at the process and created an attraction at their flagship brewery in St. Louis, which is still popular.

According to brewery officials, roughly 350,000 people toured the 142-acre complex in 2009, learning the history of Budweiser and its sister beers, seeing the brewing process and decades' worth of advertising, and ending the visit with a sample.

Until recently, most tours followed that model, but today, many breweries have taken a more hands-on approach.

Jim Koch, president of the Boston Beer Company, which produces the Samuel Adams line of beers, has for years been making an annual trip to Germany to select and harvest hops. (You may have spotted one of those excursions in a Samuel Adams commercial.) It occurred to him a few years ago that others would be interested in joining him on his trips, visiting centuries-old breweries and learning about beer in the place that perfected it. So a few years back, Boston Beer partnered with travel company Abercrombie & Kent to create a weeklong excursion to Bavaria's beer country. The itinerary included visits to various bier-gartens, the Stanglmair Farm and Hops Field just north of Munich, and the Weihenstephan Brewery, which dates back to the year 1040.

Koch told us that there were no immediate plans to do another such trip, which cost about $3,000 a person, but that his company would focus its efforts closer to home through a partnership with a luxury hotel in Boston. In addition to a stay at the hotel, participants will get a private tour of the company's Jamaica Plain neighborhood brewery, where one of the brewers will show off the facilities and lead a tasting in the barrel room, a space usually closed to the public. Samuel Adams merchandise and a beer dinner with a brewery expert are included.

"Just like baby boomers adopted wine, their kids are adopting beer, and the parallels are extraordinary and enormous," Mr. Koch told us. "People want a better experience with their beer."

But the microbreweries still offer the most intimate experiences. The Woodstock Inn, a New Hampshire brewpub, began offering week-end packages within a year after opening its brewery in 1995, both to capitalize on the growing popularity of craft beer and to drum up busi-ness during the off-season, said owner Scott Rice. Their brewer week-ends offer guests a chance to get inside the brewhouse and work on a commercial system. It's great fun and a chance for homebrewers to try their hand at something a little bigger. Guests can take part in every step of the brewing process, including the messy work of removing hundreds of pounds of processed grain from the mash tun, where grain and water are mixed.

Other breweries across the country offer similar packages with varying specifics. For example, Dogfish Head Craft Brewed Ales, a Delaware-based brewery, has partnered with a local inn where visitors are welcomed with amenities like beer soap and a library of brewing books. A tour of the brewery is also included.

In the Pacific Northwest, Rogue Ales, one of the more celebrated American craft breweries, has a six-bedroom house on its 42-acre hops farm in Independence, Oregon. Brett Joyce, president of the brewery, said that staying there gives visitors a chance to better experience one of beer's main ingredients. The farm even hosted a wedding last year. The bottom line is that beer, the people who brew it, and those who love it are not second-class citizens as some of the wine-minded people in this country might think. This is the new golden age of beer, and traveling to breweries like those found in this book gives us a better understanding of where the American beer scene has come from and where it is going.

The Hoosier Heartland
Central Indiana and Fort Wayne

Get out of the metropolis that is Indianapolis and drive through the central part of the state, where you really get to see the American heartland. While we're calling this portion of the book Central Indiana, it will really encompass more than that. We start out in Richmond on the Ohio border and zip across the state, past cornfields and farmland, and head to Kokomo and Lafayette. Later, we'll explore historic towns like Noblesville and rapidly growing ones like Greenwood.

Indiana has great highways that can easily get a person from one place to the next with very little hassle. But we often found ourselves taking slower back roads, enjoying a closer look at everyday life, unique shops, and restaurants. This is where agriculture mixes with the arts, where industry and outdoor activity combine in a unique tapestry that is distinctly Indiana.

This region is also home to some of the country's most excellent roadside attractions. In 1919, the town of Kokomo acquired a 2.5-ton, 16-foot stuffed steer named Old Ben. Legend has it Old Ben was the biggest steer in the world. You can see him in Kokomo's *Highland Park* today, right next to the sycamore stump that according to local legend is, you guessed it, the biggest sycamore stump in the world.

Near the northeast corner of the state is Fort Wayne, described to us by one resident as a place with a "small-town feel with big-city dreams." There you'll find a break from the fields. Fort Wayne was home to the first NBA team, the Pistons, who would later move to Detroit. Today, minus a major sports franchise, it remains a vibrant sports town with both minor league baseball and hockey teams that have fierce local followings and offer great contests for visitors as well.

Established during the American Revolutionary War as a group of forts under the direction of General "Mad" Anthony Wayne, the city is now the second largest in the state, behind Indianapolis.

Central Indiana also has several places that call themselves breweries, but do not fit the guidelines for this book. Ram in the town of Fishers serves beer made in the downtown Indianapolis Ram Brewery. All the brews, including seasonal beer, are delivered weekly, and the same menu and mug club deals are offered.

BJ's Restaurant and Brewhouse in Greenwood is equipped with brewing equipment, but all of its beer is shipped in from the corporate brewery in Reno, Nevada, according to a company spokesman.

There is one brewery in Central Indiana that is operational but not open to the public. Just east of Terre Haute in Brazil sits the Bee Creek Farm (www.beecreekbrewery.com), where the owners began brewing just to have spent grain on hand to feed their cattle. It's a working farm, so tours are not available, but their beer is on tap in a few places in the area and in bottles at local stores.

This part of the state is prime for diverting off the beaten path and taking a chance on a back road. You never quite know what you'll find.

So, toss the book on the front seat, get out the map, and take the back roads through the Hoosier Heartland as we experience together the best beer in the middle of the state.

Lodging in the area: We stayed at the Holiday Inn near the Indiana University–Purdue University campus (4111 Paul Shaffer Drive, Fort Wayne, 260-482-3800, www.fortwayneholidayinn.com). It is one of the more modern hotels, with comfortable amenities, close proximity to the downtown area, and staff who are friendly, professional, and make you feel like family. The hotel also partners with the hospitality program at the university, giving students real-life experience perfecting the art of hotel management. Other good options are Guesthouse Hotel, Restaurant, and Conference Center, 1313 West Washington Center Road, Fort Wayne, 260-489-2524, www.donhalls.com; Allison House, 90 South Jefferson Street, Nashville, 812-988-0814, www.allisonhouseinn.net; and Quaker Hill Conference Center, 10 Quaker Hill Drive, Richmond, 765-962-5741, www.qhcc.org. If you like to stay in a place with a more personal touch, a bed-and-breakfast is likely your best option. We found http://www.indianabedandbreakfast.org to be a good resource. Also check with the following convention and visitors bureaus: Fort Wayne,

www.visitfortwayne.com; Muncie, www.munciecvb.org; Kokomo, www
.visitkokomo.org; Eastern Indiana, www.easternindiana.com.

Area attractions: Founded by Swiss Mennonite immigrants, *Berne* is a community that has retained much of its charm and Old World style. Visit restaurants, working farms, and specialty shops and see how life was in a simpler time. In Lafayette, *Tippecanoe Battlefield* (200 Battleground Avenue, 765-476-8411, www.tcha.mus.in.us/battlefield.htm) is where the famous battle took place. Today the site features exhibits and recreational options. *The Clabber Girl Museum* in Terre Haute (900 Wabash Avenue, 812-232-9446, www.clabbergirl.com) is home to a history of kitchens, with cooking demonstrations and information on the science of baking. In Huntington, learn all about the people who held the second most important elected office in the country at the *Quayle Vice Presidential Learning Center* (815 Warren Street, 260-356-6356, www.quaylemuseum.org). Take a ride on the *CKS Railroad* (112 West Carey Street, Knightstown, 765-345-5561, www.cksrail.com), a seasonal trip along the Big Four Route that takes about seventy-five minutes to complete. Basketball is religion in Indiana, and while it's tradition to pay reverence at the hardwood of a local high school or university, it is also necessary to take a pilgrimage to the *Indiana Basketball Hall of Fame* in New Castle (408 Trojan Lane, 765-529-1891, www.hoopshall.com). For a closer look at life under the Big Top, check out the *International Circus Hall of Fame* in Peru (3076 Circus Lane, 765-472-7553, www.circushalloffame.com)

In Fort Wayne, don't miss up a chance to visit the *Genealogy Center* at Allen County Public Library (900 Library Place, 260-421-1225, www.acpl.lib.in.us/genealogy/index.html), which is perhaps the best place in the country to research and discover your family history. Set up in a user-friendly facility, the $65 million center has records dating back to the 1700s and countless materials to help you trace your family tree. Looking for something sweet? Visit *DeBrand Chocolatier* (260-969-8333, www.debrand.com), a local artisan chocolate shop that offers tours and tastings. *Fort Wayne Firefighters Museum* (226 West Washington Boulevard, 260-426-0051) is home to some early equipment used by city firefighters and highlights more than a century and a half of fighting flames. Get lost for a bit wandering the grounds of the *Foellinger-Freimann Botanical Conservatory* (1100 South Calhoon Street, 260-427-6440, www.botanicalconservatory.org), home to seasonal displays, orchids, palm trees, and a desert garden. Learn more about Fort Wayne, Gen. "Mad" Anthony Wayne, and other notable residents of the area at the *History Center* (302 East Berry Street, 260-426-2282, www.fwhistorycenter.com).

Other beer sites: Although it might seem like you have to drive long distances to find a great pint of craft beer in Central Indiana, there are several places we know you will like. *Little Sheba's Restaurant & Zini's Place* (175 Fort Wayne Avenue, Richmond, 765-962-2999, www.littleshebas.com) has the local New Boswell Brewing Company beer on tap and a selection of pizzas and sandwiches that take up several pages in an already large menu. *The Fickle Peach* (117 East Charles Street, Muncie, 765-282-5211, www.theficlepeach.com) says it's "passionately dedicated to great beer" and they deliver on the promise. Be it pints from Jolly Pumpkin in Michigan or brews from Upland in Bloomington, chances are good you'll find something excellent. *The Quarry* (2130 W. Sycamore Street, Suite 200, Kokomo, 765-450-5650, www.thequarry kokomo.com) is a fancy restaurant featuring a good selection of craft beers. Both the *Black Sparrow* (223 Main Street, Lafayette, 765-429-0405, www.blacksparrowpub.com) and *Chumley's* (122 North 3rd Street, Lafayette, 765-420-9372) are worthy places with great craft selections. *J K O'Donnell's* (121 West Wayne Street, Fort Wayne, 260-420-5563, www.jkodonnells.com) has a great tap selection in a Irish pub setting. Be sure to try the fish and chips.

People's Brewing Company

2006 N. 9th Street Road, Lafayette, IN 47904
(765) 714-2777 • www.peoplesbrew.com

Chris Johnson had the vision to create the People's Brewery even before he got his first brewery job scrubbing floors at the Lafayette Brewing Company across town.

"My goal from day one was to have my own brewery," said Johnson, who sports a dirty-blonde ponytail and mountain man beard. "That was the plan from the get-go."

Along with partner Brett Vander Plaats, brother of Johnson's wife Jessica, the People's Brewing Company made its first batch of German Pilsner on Thanksgiving Day 2009.

Located in a warehouse across North 3rd Street from the railroad tracks and next to a used car dealership, Johnson said the key to his beer's taste is the water, which is drawn from a well out back near the banks of the Wabash River. It is hard and unsoftened, similar to the water in the north of Germany, which makes it perfect for German-style beers, Johnson said. "Rather than changing the water to fit the beer, we craft the beer to fit the water," he said. Johnson added that while the brewery imports its hops, grains, and malts, they use "locally raised water."

The company also brews a hoppy American Amber and an even hoppier American IPA. Johnson describes it as "a little bit more hop-ambitious than the other beers we've got."

In winter, the brewery crafts brown ale, porter, and stout. In summer, it brews lighter English-style beers. Johnson specializes in "session beers," those with an alcohol content around 5 percent or less. Johnson said the reason is to allow drinkers to enjoy more than one without getting too "schnozzled."

Johnson apprenticed at the Lafayette Brewing Company and later was the head brewer for eight years. There he followed the recipes given to him by Lafayette owner and brewmaster Greg Emig. In the back of his mind, he formulated ideas that would become People's Brewery product.

"I wasn't being paid to innovate," Johnson said. "And I wanted my ideas in my pocket when it came to making my own beers."

The company services more than twenty accounts in Tippecanoe County, plus a few in Indianapolis and surrounding areas. While Johnson hopes to expand further, he said he wants to concentrate on getting more accounts in his home county.

Johnson and Vander Plaats deliver their beers themselves in a moving truck with the People's Brewing logo painted on the side. "If we can afford to drive it, we will," Johnson said. People's also fills growlers on location.

Johnson learned to homebrew while studying graphic design at Purdue. When he was out of college he was ready to pack up and move to brewery-rich Colorado to take any gig he could find making brews. Nearly a decade later, when the time came for him to open his own brewery, he chose to stay in Lafayette. He looked at nearly sixty locations before he settled on his warehouse.

Born and raised in rural Lagrange in the northeastern Indiana, Johnson worked on farms as a young man and now finds brewing comparable.

The Pick: Sometimes you want an original. That's why we wholeheartedly endorse the Pilsner. Taste what folks in the 1800s were experiencing and how using traditional methods makes the difference between this beer and mass-market lagers.

Beers brewed: German Pilsner, American IPA, American Amber, plus rotating seasonal beers.

"Working on farms is very hands-on, and I liked it," he said. "Brewing is very hands-on."

People's Brewing has a 20-barrel brewhouse with 40-barrel fermentation tanks, which allows Johnson to brew twice and put the brew into the same finishing tanks.

Johnson said he wants his company to be heir to the town's rich brewing heritage. Lafayette was once home to the Thieme and Wagner brewery, which made nearly a million barrels of beer a year before Prohibition. Though the company rebounded under a new owner as Lafayette Brewing Incorporated in 1933, it died again less than two decades later, the victim of refrigerated boxcars that delivered mass-produced lagers like Budweiser and Coors nationwide. It was a fate that befell many a local brewery.

"At People's we wanted to bring back the community brewery in Lafayette," Johnson said. To that end Johnson is building a bar in the brewery's tasting room from hunks of wood donated by patrons. Each piece of wood will be lacquered and hand stamped with its donor's name.

"So they'll forever have their piece of the People's bar," Johnson said.

He brims with confidence, knowing that soon he'll be brewing for a lot more people.

"Everybody likes good beer," he said. "Some just don't know it."

People's Brewing Company

Opened: December 2009

Owners: Chris Johnson, Brett Vander Plaats

Brewer: Chris Johnson

System: 20-barrel system from AAA Metal Fabrication, 40-barrel fermentation system.

Production: 700 barrels estimated for 2010.

Brewpub hours: Wednesday through Saturday, 12 P.M. to 7 P.M.; Sunday, 11 A.M. to 3 P.M.

Take-out beer: Growlers

Tours: By appointment or walks-ins accepted.

Special considerations: Handicapped-accessible

Parking: Free lot

Mad Anthony Brewing Company

2002 Broadway, Fort Wayne, IN 46802
260-426-ALES (2537) • www.madbrew.com

In the 1990s, as the microbrewery movement gained momentum, Blaine Stuckey and Todd Grantham decided to go into business together and open their own brewery in their hometown of Fort Wayne.

They quit their jobs, and Todd headed down to Oaken Barrel Brewing Company in Greenwood as an assistant brewer to learn that end of the business, while Blaine got into a restaurant management program. A year later when the owner of an eatery called Munchies wanted to sell, Blaine and Todd each took out a second mortgage on their houses, took a deep breath, and purchased the business. After another year and a half, they opened a small brewhouse. Their brew room had been used to make ice cream when the building previously housed a pharmacy. Todd and Blaine soon began selling directly to businesses around town, personally handling each account.

Fifteen years later it appears the gamble has paid off. They've added a production brewery in a large warehouse in the brewpub parking lot and have opened up three other taproom-restaurants under the Mad Anthony name in the northern part of Indiana.

On the day we were supposed to meet Blaine at the brewery, he was running late. So we settled into the bar and met Rose, the bartender.

"We'll just play beer until he gets here," she said. She then put nine different beer samples down and expertly explained each one.

As we tasted our way through the Gabby Blonde, a solid wheat beer, to the chocolate cherry stout, brewed with Belgian chocolate and tart Michigan cherries, Rose started showing us the glassware. There were the standard pints, of course, but the growlers were really captivating. They have one, a swing top, which Rose called the "I Dream of Jeanie" bottle, because with all the curves and lines, it does indeed look like a genie's bottle. For their standard growler, Mad Anthony partnered with Acres, a local conservatory group

The Pick: If you're lucky enough to visit in the fall, you won't want to miss the Oktoberfest Lager. True to the German style, it's a hearty brew that demands an oompah band and lederhosen.

Beers brewed: Harry Baal's Irish Stout, Gabby Blonde Lager, Ol' Woody Pale Ale, Auburn Lager, and Raspberry Wheat. Also about fifty other seasonals, so you never quite know what you'll find on tap.

looking to preserve lands in and around Fort Wayne. A dollar from each growler sold goes to the charity.

When you find a beer sample that you like—one you really, really like—you can order the boot. Handmade in Europe and etched with the Mad Anthony logo, the boot can hold 84 ounces of delicious fermented beverage. "It's more for a group," Blaine said when he arrived, "but there have been some solo attempts as well."

Over lunch we talked about how Indiana's beer culture has evolved in recent years. There is more of a demand for locally made products now, but it's still tough to break people of tradition. That's evidenced in the main dining room ceiling, where you can see hundreds upon hundreds of names painted in white. Those brave, mostly college-aged, patrons earned the honor after successfully drinking twelve Heineken bottles in one sitting. In the kitchen, the name of a recent Fort Wayne mayor can be seen.

These days, Heineken is still available in bottles behind the bar, but the ceiling immortality is no longer bestowed, nor is consuming that much of the Amsterdam brew recommended. Blaine and Todd have begun adding other Indiana brewery offerings in bottles—Lafayette, Three Floyds, Mishawaka—and hope to wean down their selection of conglomerate-owned or mass-produced beers in the coming years.

Their own beers are the only ones available on draft. Mad Anthony's brews several year-round beers including the Blonde, Amber, IPA, and a stout. They also have rotating seasonals or often, whatever the brewer felt like making.

When they started, Blaine said they reached out to as many businesses as possible and had accounts with chain restaurants that operated nationally, like T.G.I Friday's, but as time went on, they refocused their efforts and these days you'll still find their beer on tap at locally owned places.

Same with menu items. They get their buffalo meat from local farms and much of their seafood from a local hatchery. "Local has been our focus and it's been fantastic," Blaine said. As much as Mad Anthony is about the American entrepreneurial spirit, it's also about loving what you do and doing what you love.

"We just want to make beer," said Blaine "This is our retirement."

Mad Anthony Brewing Company

Opened: 1998
Owners: Blaine Stuckey, Todd Grantham, Jeff Neels
Brewer: Todd Grantham

Tours: By appointment

System: 7-barrel Cross, 15-barrel mono bloc

Production: 2,200 barrels estimated for 2010.

Brewpub hours: Monday, Friday, and Saturday, 11 A.M. to midnight; Tuesday through Thursday, 11 A.M. to 11 P.M.; Sunday, 11 A.M. to 10 P.M.

Take-out beer: Growlers, bottles

Food: American pub fare

Extras: Live music once or twice a week

Special considerations: Handicapped-accessible

Parking: Ample parking in lot

Lafayette Brewing Company

622 Main Street, Lafayette, IN 47901
(765) 742-2591 • www.lafayettebrewingco.com

Back in 1993, Greg Emig thought that business at his new venture in downtown Lafayette, the town's first local brewery in more than forty years, would start slow and eventually pick up. When he opened on the first day, there was a line of two hundred people out his door. "We were, quite frankly, overwhelmed beyond belief," Emig said.

Today the Lafayette Brewing Company remains as popular as ever, heralded around Lafayette and West Lafayette, home of Purdue University, for its hearty food, music, and its stable of beers.

When it opened that Friday in September 1993, the Lafayette Brewing Company was one of only three microbreweries in the state of Indiana, and it was the state's first restaurant and brewery built in the same room after a law passed that year allowing the two establishments to be connected. The other two, Broad Ripple Brewing Company and Mishawaka Brewing Company, both served food, but by law their kitchens were not connected to their breweries.

The Pick: The Eastside Bitter is a perfect balance of hops and malt. Don't let the name fool you, this is a delicious beer that gets better with each pint.

Beers brewed: Ouiatenon Wit Beer, Prophet's Rock Pale Ale, Eastside Bitter, Piper's Pride, Tippecanoe Common Ale, Eighty-Five, Black Angus Oatmeal Stout.

Emig and his wife Nancy both attended Purdue University. There, Emig began homebrewing. "My wife likes to say I'm a homebrewer gone mad," Emig said. "It got to the point where the hobby was all consuming. I always knew someday I'd want to open my own business."

The Emigs scoured the Midwest from Cincinnati to Kansas City for a downtown location in a college town to set up shop. The fates nudged them back toward their alma mater when the pet food company Nancy Emig worked for in Lawrence, Kansas, transferred her back to Lafayette in 1989. Meanwhile, Greg had learned the craft of brewing working at Free State Brewing Company in Lawrence and Broad Ripple Brewing Company in Indianapolis.

The couple found that the property on Main Street in Lafayette met their needs. The building had been constructed in 1892 and for much of its existence functioned as a furniture factory and store. In the early days, Emig and his wife lived in a cavernous loft on the building's second floor with no hot water and a broken window that let in snowdrifts.

The brewery's top seller is the Tippecanoe Common Ale, which Emig started making in 1998. At a beer convention in Chicago, he had discovered Amarillo hops, which are grown in the Pacific Northwest rather than Texas, and began using them as an ingredient. "It was a hop I knew I wanted to produce a beer out of," Emig said. "By 1999, it was our flagship."

The brewery's second-best seller is the Black Angus Oatmeal Stout, which was the second batch of beer Emig made at the Lafayette Brewing Company. The company's first brew, an American pale ale crossed with an extra special bitter named E's Original Bathtub Ale, was discontinued after about six months, but every year a few people still request it, Emig said.

Originally, Lafayette was called Tippecanoe Brewing Company, after the county in which it is located. Emig, however, received a cease and desist order from a lawyer representing the Oldenburg Brewing Company in Fort Mitchell, Kentucky, because it was operating a contract brew of the same name.

Emig had shied away from the name Lafayette Brewing, as the town's once-legendary Theme and Wagner brewery was renamed Lafayette Brewing Incorporated after it reopened under new ownership after Prohibition. It closed again less than twenty years later.

Emig said he called descendants of the Thieme and Wagner families and asked if he could use the name Lafayette Brewing. They were flattered, he said. Today, a few of them are patrons of his. "Which is really cool," Emig said.

Many Thieme and Wagner artifacts decorate the walls at Lafayette Brewing Company, including an old tap box from Lafayette Brewing Incorporated and the framed liquor permit granted to the company on the day Prohibition ended—April 7, 1933.

Emig filled the cavernous interior with rustic-looking pine, trying to create "an American brewpub," he said. The bar area and main dining area are separated by a wooden wall lined with coasters from beer breweries all over the world. "People just brought them in," Emig said. "We had to do something with them."

Other decorations include wooden statues of a Native American, the Purdue mascot Boiler Pete, and English characters, such as a cricket player and a constable.

The downstairs bar is L-shaped, with a copper top and an oak edge. The beers are poured from two brass, mushroom-shaped taps. They are antiques that were once used by Chicago's Burghoff Brewery.

The bar in the cavernous second floor, where Lafayette hosts concerts, is oval shaped and has a full liquor menu. The room also features pool tables and foosball.

Lafayette has a full menu, printed like a newspaper, that features a mix of European and American pub food, including scrumptious Bavarian beer nuggets and a double bison burger, with meat from buffalos raised at a nearby ranch.

The taps also pour the brewery's wit beer (Ouiatenon), pale ale (Prophet's Rock), bitter (East Side), Scottish ale (Piper's Pride), and American ale (Eighty-Five). They also serve up seasonal beers and cask ales.

Lafayette features a mug club for members, and the mugs themselves are handcrafted from clay and stacked behind the bar.

Jessica Johnson, wife of People's Brewery owner Chris Johnson, worked at Lafayette Brewing Company along with her husband for years. She said the establishment would always have a place in her heart.

"Greg brews a good ol' beer," she said. "I love this place. It will always be my local."

Emig said his goal today remains the same as at Lafayette's inception. "First and foremost our job is to educate the community into different beer styles," he said. "There's more to the beer community than American lagers and American light lagers."

Lafayette Brewing Company

Opened: September 1993

Owners: Greg and Nancy Emig

Brewer: Matt Williams

System: 7-barrel system from Century Manufacturing Inc.; six fermenters.

Production: 800 barrels in 2009, 800 barrels estimated for 2010.

Brewpub hours: Monday through Thursday, 11 A.M. to midnight; Friday and Saturday, 11 A.M. to 1 A.M. Kitchen is open until 11 P.M. daily.

Take-out beer: Growlers, 1/12 kegs, bottles of Common Ale and Oatmeal Stout

Tours: By appointment

Food: American pub fare

Extras: Live music upstairs

Special considerations: Handicapped-accessible

Parking: On street

Half Moon Restaurant & Brewery

4051 S. Lafountain Street, Kokomo, IN 46902
(765) 455-BREW (2739)
www.halfmoonbrewery.com

Craft beer brewers are as varied as they are colorful.

They share a common commitment to a craft and a lifestyle. They have chosen a career path that sets them outside the sobering norm of nine-to-fivers. They also realize they are unlikely to get rich practicing their vocation, but they do it anyway. Like artists.

Also like artists, what brewers make can represent their personality. Perhaps nowhere in Indiana is this truer than at Kokomo's Half Moon Restaurant & Brewery, where John Templet makes the liquid gold.

John came to the Midwest via northern California and the Deep South. "Life just takes you directions and you just keep going with it," he said with a Creole accent and a Berkeley attitude.

Just as John's hint of a drawl masks the time that slips away in conversation with him, so too do the sweet honey notes of his brilliantly named The KokoMonster disguise its 8.1 percent alcohol wallop.

"When I first brewed it, people were literally falling out of their chairs," John said. "But they kept asking, 'When are you going to make more?' So I went a little overboard."

John's humor, while charming, has just a drop of risqué and is on display on the bar wall. To the left of the taps is a photo of him from behind, pants a couple sips shy of the brim, bent over to tend his brewing tanks. Half moon, get it?

With similar salt, he named one of the brewery's best selling beers the MILF-n-Honey-Wheat, MILF being an acronym for an expression about an attractive woman of a certain age that is best not explained in these pages.

"It was time to make a light beer, a chick beer," John said. "So I thought, milk and honey, MILF and honey. It just rolls off the tongue."

Half Moon opened in March 2007. Owner Chris Roegner went to Taylor High School, just outside of Kokomo, and went on to play football at Purdue. His father, Don Roegner, a psychologist, collects classic beer memorabilia from around the region, some of which is on display in Half Moon's foyer, including beer boxes from the Burghoff brewery and shelves full of colorful, old-fashioned beer cans.

The walls are decorated with old photos of Kokomo, newspapers with tornado headlines, pictures of the old Haynes and Apperson car manufacturing plant, and a shot of the Drapper Brothers' Brewery. It was one of two breweries in Kokomo near the turn of the twentieth century. Both were gone by the time the Wright brothers flew.

Half Moon's beers are all named in honor of local landmarks and celebrities, said manager Chris Salinas. The Cannon Shot Cream is named for a nearby ammunition factory. The Wildcat Wheat is after Wildcat Creek, which meanders through the fields. Stoplight City Red acknowledges one of Kokomo's nicknames, given because of the galling number of red signals downtown, Salinas said.

The Hazlenut Brown used to be named Old Ben Brown after the enormous stuffed bull on display in Kokomo's Highland Park. Next to the toro taxidermy sits what's left of an enormous sycamore tree chopped down by early settlers. From it, Half Moon got the name for its darkest beer, the Sycamore Stump Oatmeal Stout, Salinas said.

Elwood's IPA is named for Elwood Haynes, who helped build the first automobile. That prototype car earned Kokomo another nickname, City of Firsts. Half Moon tweaked it to City of Thirsts.

The Pick: KokoMonster. Too many and it will destroy you. Clocking in at 8.1 percent ABV, this Old Ale will knock you down and carry you into the woods before you know what hit you. That's not necessarily a bad thing, until the next morning.

Beers brewed: Cole Porter, Elwood's IPA, Hazelnut Brown Ale, Stoplight City Red, Wildcat Wheat, Cannon Shot Cream Ale, MILF-n-Honey-Wheat Ale, KokoMonster.

Half Moon further secures its reputation for clever wordplay with a brew named after a famous jazz composer who was born eighteen miles north of Kokomo in Peru. The beer is simply called Cole Porter.

There are seasonal brews on tap as well. All beers are available in growler size. Half Moon features a mug club, which gives members discounts on beer, invitations to keg tappings, and deals on dishes from the restaurant's hearty, heartland menu.

The lofty interior is brick. The bar itself is a polished oak slab atop aluminum siding. There are plenty of flatscreens around. During the football playoffs, each time the Colts scored, the house bought the patrons a round of Apple Pie shots. That's Everclear and apple juice for you mixologists.

"We strive so hard to make sure that the vibe you get here is welcoming," Salinas said. "And makes you want to come back."

Fergus Beedham, a gymnastics instructor from the United Kingdom, brought it to the owners' attention that there is a pub also called the Half Moon in a village on the east coast of England. Beedham facilitated a souvenir exchange between the two establishments. Today they swap recipes.

"I come here for the beer, it's as simple as that," said Beedham, a regular. "It was hard to resist as an Englishman."

Brewer John Templet was born in Baton Rouge, Louisiana. He grew up between his red dirt birthplace and Mendocino, California. Unlike many brewers, he said that in college he didn't make his own beer. "But I drank a lot of it," he admitted. In 1992, he took a job as a dishwasher at the Mendocino Brewing Company in Hopland, California. Eventually, he worked his way up to brewmaster and held the position for eight years.

"That's where I learned about beer," he said. "I didn't know what it was all about at first, but I fell in love with it."

John then went on to Little Rock, Arkansas, where he brewed at the Diamond Bear Brewing Company. Later he took a job at Bosco's, billed as a restaurant for beer lovers, in Memphis. After a year he was transferred back to Little Rock to help open a new Bosco's location where Little Rock's River Rock Brewing used to be. In Little Rock, John married musician Kristy Templet, who toured with musical theater shows. She got a lead on a job at a dinner theatre at Beef and Board's in Indianapolis and, wanting to get off the road, set about trying to find her husband a job as a Hoosier brewer.

At Half Moon she found a home for both his brewing skills and his humor.

Reflecting on the popularity of his MILF-n-Honey-Wheat brew, John drawls, "I could pee in it and it would still sell."

Half Moon Restaurant & Brewery

Owner: Chris Roegner
Brewer: John Templet
System: 3¹/₂-barrel system from Pub Brewing Company, 7-barrel fermenter.
Production: 380 barrels in 2009, 500 barrels estimated for 2010.
Brewpub hours: Daily, 11 A.M. to 11 P.M.
Take-out beer: Growlers
Tours: By appointment
Food: American fare, featuring smokehouse meats and weekly specials.
Extras: Trivia nights on Mondays, food and beer pairings on Thursdays, live TV poker.
Special considerations: Handicapped-accessible.
Parking: Free lot.

Barley Island Brewing Company

639 Conner Street (Highway 32)
Noblesville, IN 46060
(317) 770-5280 • www.barleyisland.com

At times it can seem like the highways and roads around the Indianapolis metro area offer views of one suburban strip after another. McDonald's, Auto Zone, Home Depot, Walgreens, Applebees, and every other national chain seem to flow into another strip with nearly identical stores.

Make the turn onto Noblesville's Conner Street from Indiana State Road 37, however, and you are greeted with a true American Main Street. Stately homes, locally owned businesses, and on the corner of South 6th Street, Barley Island Brewing. The building itself dates back to 1890, and it served as a beer distributor from 1933, the year Prohibition was repealed, until the 1980s. In 1999, Jeff and Linda Eaton took ownership of the building and opened a brewpub.

From the moment we walked in, history was in the air. The solid wood bar looks like it has been around since Noblesville was incorporated, and the dim winter light coming in the front windows gave the place a serene feeling. Because we were the only people in the place, it was easy to find a spot at the bar—salvaged from an Irish pub that once stood in Brownsburg—and we were greeted by a friendly server who was happy to put a sampler down in front of us.

We found all the beers to be a near-perfect representation of the style. Each was a great session beer in its own way. They also serve a root beer that was probably like our grandparents drank as kids at the local drug store. Barley Island will even fill a growler with the sassafras-flavored soda.

The menu is typical fare—burgers, wraps, and sandwiches—but it is vegetarian friendly, with nearly a dozen non-meat options, a rare find in Central Indiana.

When we visited they had guest taps from Indiana's New Albanian Brewing Company and Victory Brewing of Pennsylvania. The fridge also had bottles from Big Sky Brewing in Montana and Left Hand of Colorado. Those came from regular customers looking to share their unique-to-Indiana finds with friends and fellow beer enthusiasts alike.

The place is packed on weekends, when local music acts set up in a corner of the dining room. We're told there is usually a line for the ancient Asteroid arcade game in the corner.

The brewery is attached to the restaurant and patrons in the dining room can see the fermentation tanks through a window. Jeff and Linda have been busy since they opened a taproom in Indianapolis's Broad Ripple neighborhood in 2009, so we weren't able to get a tour. We were, however, glad to enjoy a few pints of their hard work.

The Pick: Dirty Helen Brown is a good session beer that most everyone can appreciate. Also pairs well with a burger, pizza, or just about anything else on the menu. Plus, it's available in bottles around the state for at-home enjoyment.

Beers brewed: 80 Shilling Scotch Ale, Brass Knuckles Oatmeal Stout, BarFly IPA, Dirty Helen Brown Ale, Beastie Barrel Porter, Flat Top Wheat, Rust Belt Porter, Blind Tiger Pale Ale

Barley Island Brewing Company

Opened: 1999

Owners: Jeff and Linda Eaton

Brewpub hours: Monday through Thursday, 11 A.M. to midnight; Friday and Saturday, 11 A.M. to 1 A.M.; Sunday, 3 P.M. to midnight.

Take-out beer: Bottles, growlers

Food: American pub fare

Extras: Live music on occasion

Special considerations: Handicapped-accessible

Parking: Free lot

Big Woods Brewing Company

60 Molly Lane, Nashville, IN 47448
(812) 988-6000 • www.bigwoodsbeer.com

Nashville can be tough to navigate for first timers. Nearly all the streets are one way and buildings are so tight against the roadways that cars come dangerously close to them. When we came upon Big Woods Brewing Company, the chef, Emily Stone, greeted us while standing outside at a Weber grill. She had just tossed a burger and large portabella mushroom on the fire, and we asked her to do the same for us.

It became clear after spending only a few minutes inside the Big Woods Brewing Company that one of Indiana's newest brewpubs is a family affair. In fact you might need a family tree or a flowchart to see how everyone is connected.

Launched in late 2009 by Jeff McCabe, Ed Ryan, and Tim O'Bryan, the brewery was in need of employees, so the owners quickly enlisted other family members and friends to help out with things. For starters, brewer Tim is Jeff's son-in-law. On our first visit, we found Jeff's sister-in-law, Spring (who goes by the title of Goddess on her business card), busy pouring house beers, taking orders, and dropping off plates, while at the same time giving us the history of the place and making us feel like we were old friends.

In a small town like Nashville, it is good to have friends and family close by and Jeff told us that he used the talents of many during the planning and construction phase. From the wood framing to the iron and electrical work, Jeff and company used local businesses, contactors, and anyone else willing to grab a hammer and get to work.

"Everything we've done to get here is a collaboration and inspired by those relationships," Jeff said.

Even the materials used in the construction come from local sources, including the bar itself, which is made from Indiana limestone, and the wooden tap handles, crafted by a local woodworker. After all, Nashville is an artists' colony

The Pick: Tim's Big Woods Stout is served on nitro (just like Guinness) and pours a creamy black with good flavor from the black patent malts that give it a mild roasted chocolate flavor and nice finish.

Beers brewed: Tim's Big Woods Stout, Busted Knuckle Red, Possum Trot Pale Ale, Six Foot Blonde.

and the Big Woods wanted to stay true to form. Jeff is sure to give credit where it is due and has printed up bar cards with all the names of the people and local businesses that made the brewery a reality as a token of thanks.

The name Big Woods comes from the fact that Nashville is surrounded by forests, perfect for a day of hiking or bike riding, and the brewpub is great because it gives you a chance to get your quaff on after a full day of exercise.

When Big Woods first opened, its restaurant was closed on Mondays and Tuesdays, so that Tim could set up his equipment in the kitchen, brew, and then dismantle. Since then, an addition to the building has given Tim a place to call his own. That has made life easier in the woods and allows the kitchen to be open seven days a week. Tim, in turn, now brews about four times a week to keep up with demand.

His now shed-sized brewery houses a one-barrel system with which he can tweak a few of the beers, like the stout and the blonde, to levels that make him happier. Customers, too, have few complaints.

The family aspect of the place is confirmed when you enter the restaurant itself. It's small, with only a handful of tables and a few seats at the bar. It feels like you're in a family dining room.

There is a television set behind the bar, but mercifully it wasn't on just for the sake of being on. When we visited, we enjoyed looking around and seeing people packed into every table and barstool chatting among themselves, taking long silent stretches to enjoy the food and wash it down with a pint.

What sealed it for us was the bathroom. Off to the side of the bar, the co-ed toilet is filled with pictures of brewery staff, friends, and plenty of construction shots. There is even a stocked bookshelf and some magazines to help pass the time. You too can leave your mark by signing the back of the door, which has its own blackboard and complimentary chalk. Leave a message for the next person, but keep it polite. This is a family restaurant after all.

Big Woods Brewing Company

Opened: 2009

Owners: Jeff McCabe, Ed Ryan, Tim O'Bryan

Brewer: Tim O'Bryan

Brewpub hours: Monday through Thursday, 11:30 A.M. to 9 P.M.; Friday to Saturday, 11:30 A.M. to 11 P.M.; Sunday, 11:30 A.M. to 7 P.M.

Take-out beer: Growlers

Food: Hearty pub food with local flavor.

Special considerations: Handicapped-accessible

Parking: Street parking is tough in Nashville, but it's available. There are also several pay lots in the area.

Wilbur BrewHause

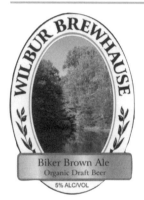

2548 W. Forest Lake Lane, Martinsville, IN 46151
(765) 346-0023 • www.wilburbrewco.com

The hand-painted sign told us it was a private road, but the GPS urged us on. Making the left from the paved road, we found the car suddenly on gravel. Grumbling forward, we made one more turn and eventually found ourselves literally in the driveway of a house.

Exiting the car, the first thing we heard was bleating. To the left there was a goat staring impassively at us. A few dogs were penned in to the side and all around was the stillness of a forest and a modest two-story home ahead.

Of all the breweries in the state of Indiana, this has to be the most intimate. We walked to the front door and rang the bell. Dan Hause, owner and brewer of the Wilbur BrewHause, answered and led us around the house where his land truly revealed itself. His house had been blocking the real view—the property triangles into a pristine lake and near the edge of the water is a red-painted A-frame cabin, home to the brewery.

The neighborhood was once a Girl Scout camp, Hause explained while opening the brewery door. This was one of the last remaining cabins from those days, and he and his family used the property as a weekend getaway until they finally built the main house a few years back. The goat? That's to eat the poison ivy that grows on the property.

A while back Dan bought his son a homebrew kit and together they brewed up a batch of an Oktoberfest-style lager. They let it ferment in the rafters of the son's house where the temperature

The Pick: Dan has a summer seasonal that is crisp, refreshing, and carries a hell of a punch. It's not one to quaff when the weather is hot, but it makes for a nice relief at the end of a hard day.

Beers brewed: Country Mellow, Biker Brown Ale.

was most agreeable for the time of year. It didn't turn out half bad, according to Dan, so they continued to brew, sharing with friends and family along the way.

His son eventually gave up the craft, but Dan continued, and as he neared his retirement began thinking of the next phase of his life. Brewing beer, he decided, wasn't too hard and he enjoyed it. So, he incorporated, got some larger equipment, and looked for a niche.

He found it 25 miles to the south in Bloomington. The ultimate Indiana college town is home to an eclectic group of students, professors, and families, and their tastes vary. Dan noticed, however, a big organic food movement and looked into making an organic brew.

He uses malt extract and whole hops. Even his cleaning equipment is certified. As such, his bottled beer carries a USDA Certified Organic label. "The stores in Bloomington wanted something that was local and organic and I am both," he said.

We started a tasting with Dan pouring three different beers: his Country Mellow, Biker Brown, and a summer ale. Each had a complexity that was beyond homebrewing, but not as polished as some of the larger breweries. That wasn't a bad thing. Each felt like a comfortable beer, something slightly familiar but still new to the palate.

For his Country Mellow, which started out as a stout but is now in an unidentifiable category, Dan pulled out a clear plastic bag of Nugget hops. It's what gives the beer its unique flavor without immediately identifying itself as the vegetation.

Then he said something that very few modern American brewers say.

"I'm not a huge fan of hops. They have their place in beer, but I don't need to be knocked over the head with it."

Say again?

"I'd rather taste the malts; that's where I look for flavor."

And it works. His beers have a great malt character and it makes for a pleasant drinking experience.

The brewery itself isn't much. Tucked inside the cabin, he keeps the yeast in a college-dormitory-sized refrigerator, two four-barrel fermentation tanks are in a dining area, and the living room is filled with bottles and inventory. He brews the beer on a modified wood-fired, cast-iron potbelly stove, with a few loose bricks around the edge to give the two-barrel kettle a lift.

An engineer by trade, Dan has been talking with some local metal workers to come up with a new system. It reminded us of Jack McAuliffe, who launched the first American microbrewery in California in 1976. At that time, small-scale equipment did not exist commercially, so he needed to either salvage old dairy equipment or weld his own. McAuliffe once told me, "farmers make wine, engineers make beer."

In the case of Dan Hause, that's very true. He hopes to move into a larger, more appropriate space down the road and have a restaurant attached. But in the meantime, the brewery sits in close proximity to Shangri-La.

Standing on the back deck of the cabin, next to the stove, we stared out over the water. The hum of cicadas was strong, occasionally dying down with the sound of wind through the leaves. Geese could be heard in the far distance, and occasionally the cry of that goat. This brewery, for the moment, was completely void of the sounds of man. We came for the beer, we'd stay for the view . . . and another beer.

Wilbur BrewHause

Opened: July 2009
Owner: Dan Hause
Brewer: Dan Hause
System: 2 to 4 barrel fermenters
Production: 50 barrels estimated for 2010.
Tours: By appointment
Take-out beer: Growlers, bottles
Special considerations: Handicapped-accessible
Parking: On site

New Boswell Brewing Company

413 North 8th Street, Richmond, IN 47374
(765) 546-7856 • www.newboswell.com

If you drive around the country enough, you'll eventually come to a city like Richmond. Industry has long since vanished in this once-big factory town, but the residents who remained are trying their best to rehab the area and find new ways to entice businesses and residents to either move in or stay. The downtown depot project is one such attempt. Warehouses and storefronts long since abandoned are getting new lives in the form of loft apartments, specialty shops, and designer retail, anything really that will bring people in.

So, when two young Indiana University graduates expressed interest in opening up a microbrewery, the folks in charge of redevelopment jumped at the chance. Not only because it would mean a new tenant for an old space, but because of the demographic associated with craft beer: young people.

The first brewery to open in Indiana was the Boswell Brewing Company of Richmond. Fittingly enough, it was owned by a man named Boswell. Not much is known about Boswell, except that he had a mutilated eye. His business was not very successful, and it closed after only a few years. Still, it was the first and it has remained a source of pride among locals, despite the town's strong roots in the Temperance movement. Until now, the last brewery to operate in town had been shuttered since Prohibition.

Enter newlyweds and homebrewers Rodrick and Kiera Landess, who decided that they would put a business plan they first conceived in college into action. They called their venture the *New* Boswell Brewing Company. Following the brewery's namesake, Rodrick wore an eye patch, the same accessory that all characters wear in New Boswell advertisements, logos, and promotional material.

Situated in a railroad-style retail space on the corner of North 8th Street and Elm Place, the brewery is sprawling, nearly taking up the full length of a city block. New Boswell was brewing when we visited, but was also still in the construction phase as well. As such, the brewery was organized chaos. The ultimate plan calls for a homebrewing supply shop in the storefront, then a tasting room, and behind that the brewery.

There are limitations to the space, as Rodrick pointed out, including the fact that the operation is on the second floor; while it's reinforced, the weight of the beer in the four three-barrel fermentation tanks, combined with a few dozen quarter-sized kegs, was about the most the floor could handle without Rodrick worrying about finding his brewery in the basement one morning.

While far from professional, the brewing system is pretty inventive. Rather than going with a normal brewkettle, Rodrick is using a giant coffeemaker—literally a bottom-fired coffeemaker, capable of producing 60 gallons, or about 1,200 cups of coffee, and made by the J. H.

The Pick: By default it's the Cream Ale. It's really the only beer they currently make on a continuous basis. It's a crisp, refreshing beer that will help bring megabrewery beer drinkers to the craft side.

Beers brewed: New Boswell Cream Ale, New Boswell Brown Ale, New Boswell Red Ale, New Boswell Amber Ale

McKie Company of Los Angeles. It once belonged to a Masonic temple in Muncie; one of their forward-thinking members put the item up on a brewing website, thinking that the old caffeine-juice machine might serve a greater purpose in a new home.

Rodrick smiles when he talks about the machine, which is consistently percolating suds these days, but he longs for a real system and keeps an eye on the brewing boards for something a little more upscale.

The brewery originally had grand ideas of making a few different beers. After they went to market, however, the verdict came back that the cream ale was the most popular. Because of system limitations, every third batch is brewed in a different style. Rodrick has done brown ales and Irish-style red ales, but he keeps going back to the cream ale. "It's as close to a domestic pilsner as we could be without being ashamed," Rodrick explained.

We left the brewery and wound up at a pub down the street where his beer was on tap. Rodrick and Kiera weren't exactly set up for visitors when we arrived and there were no samples to be had in house.

Just by taking the quick walk from the brewery to the pub, it was clear to see that Richmond is a pretty cool town. Signs of life are peeking out from old storefronts, people with smiles on their faces walk the street, and shopkeepers stand in doorways nodding hello to passersby. There is also a public art project in town to paint murals on the sides of old brick buildings, much in the way advertisers did before billboards. There is one for the record shop and another for a kitchen supply store.

New Boswell hopes to have a mural of their own someday, and so long as the community continues to give their hometown brewery their support and business, they'll be immortalized in paint pretty soon.

New Boswell Brewing Company

Opened: 2010
Owners: Rodrick and Kiera Landess
Brewer: Rodrick Landess
System: 2$^1/_2$ barrel system; direct-fire gas kettle.
Production: 200 barrels estimated for 2010.
Tours: By appointment
Take-out beer: Growlers
Special considerations: Handicapped-accessible
Parking: Street

Oaken Barrel Brewing Company

OAKEN BARREL
50 Airport Parkway, Greenwood, IN 46143
(317) 887-2287 • www.oakenbarrel.com

The outside of the building that houses Oaken Barrel Brewing Company looks like an Old West saloon out of a John Wayne movie. Inside, however, it's clearly a sports bar. Televisions are tuned to ESPN, waitresses wear football jerseys on game days, and generous nacho platters are served. It's also a great neighborhood bar, and regulars simply call it the Oak.

A friendly server greeted us and poured a glass of the Indiana Amber while we perused the menu—sandwiches, pasta dishes, burgers, all stuff that you would expect from a family restaurant. There's something to please even the pickiest of eaters.

The beers are courtesy of Mark Havens, who has kept the quality up on the Oak's year-round beers, like the Razz-Wheat and Snake Pit Porter, but has also added some delicious and inventive brews to the mix.

In particular, he's been making roasted coffee stouts of varying flavors. A while back he did a blueberry coffee stout that was creamy, flavorful, strong, and delicious. For a first pint of the day, it's a perfect eye-opener.

It was pretty quiet at the bar when we visited, save for some regulars in the corner, nursing impressive 20-ounce mugs. Why were they so lucky? "They are mug club members," our waitress replied.

Ah, the mug club. This now-common staple of most brewpubs rewards regulars for frequent patronage. Often the reward comes with a discount. Other benefits can include invitations to tappings, special beer dinners, meal discounts, or free logo merchandise. Plus, there is the general feeling of belonging, a way of saying, "I come here a lot. They know my name."

Mug clubs are a great way to get more from a brewpub experience. Often the gatherings hosted for members turn into jolly conversations about homebrewing, beer travel, or unique brews found in local stores. Over time, strangers become friends.

We would have added the Oak to our repertoire of mug clubs, but limited space means limited mugs, and we were told there was a waiting

The Pick: Your best bet is to see which coffee stout Mark Havens has on tap and go with that. By using fresh-roasted coffee, Havens has created beers so good you'll want to start your day with them.

Beers brewed: Indiana Amber, Razz-Wheat, Gnaw Bone, Alabaster, Snake Pit Porter, Superfly, plus many seasonals.

list. So we had to rely on an insider for the real scoop on the Oak's mug club.

"You get e-mail invites to special events, including the annual Pork of July pig roast and the Super Bowl party," explained Vic Ryckaert, one of the mug club chosen. "They also tell you what's on tap and when the special brews will be available. The fall season's Apple Buzz and PumKwang Ale are my favorites and they always run out quick."

Oaken Barrel has been bottling its beers for years. Their product can be found at most package stores in the Indianapolis area. It's a source of local pride for many, and it's clear to see why there is such a waiting list among the regulars to a chance to belong to the mug club.

Opened: 1994

Owner: Kwan Casey

Brewer: Mark Havens

Brewpub hours: Monday through Thursday, 11 A.M. to midnight; Friday and Saturday, 11 A.M. to 1 A.M.; Sunday, 11 A.M. to 10 P.M.

Take-out beer: Bottles, growlers

Food: Nouveau-American cuisine, with a wide variety of salads and sandwiches.

Special considerations: Handicapped-accessible

Parking: Free lot

Black Swan Brewpub

2076 E. Hadley Road, Plainfield, IN 46168
(317) 838-7444 • www.blackswanbrewpub.com

D. J. McAllister came up through the brewing ranks, having started at the very bottom. The summer before his senior year in college he got a job washing kegs at Greenville's Oaken Barrel Brewing Company. It's typically a thankless job but a necessary one.

He progressed into home brewing, where he experimented with different recipes and carefully honed his skills. After college he scored a job at Lafayette Brewing where again he was tasked with cleaning kegs, emptying the mash tun, and "general sanitation" as he calls it. But

Lafayette's Greg Emig saw something in the young McAllister: in 1997 he offered him a job and a chance to brew.

All along, said McAllister, he held thoughts of one day owning his own place. He eventually left Lafayette Brewing and held jobs in a few different industries before winding up in Chicago to finish his MBA.

"I was saving pennies all along the way," he told us recently. When an opportunity arose to come back to Indiana and Indianapolis he realized it was time to finally open his own place. Naturally, opening any new business during the recession of 2009 was nearly impossible; McAllister, who wanted to open in downtown Indianapolis, saw several deals fall through.

That's when his tale took a positive turn. With a little hustle and some good timing, McAllister stumbled upon a location in Plainfield, an Indianapolis suburb.

"It was almost magical," he recalled. "From day one things just started working out."

Anyway, along the way, McAllister had the name "black swan" kicking around in the back of his head. The business school graduate was thinking about a book by Nassim Nicholas Taleb called *Black Swan*, which showcases the influence of improbable and unpredictable events that have a big impact.

This space he found in Plainfield had just about everything he was looking for in terms of the kitchen. The sale also included the tables and chairs, and the layout was perfect for both a brewery side and a restaurant side without the two butting against each other. Then, when D. J. and his staff started doing test runs in the kitchen, the chef was doing a lot of random pairings that just worked; McAllister again thought to the black swan. So, that became the name of his new venture into craft beer.

The brewpub once housed a restaurant that catered to the motorcycle crowd but today has an American/English pub feel. What is most impressive are the eighteen taps behind the bar.

When they opened the kitchen in the autumn of 2010, McAllister did not yet have his brewing equipment in place, but wanted to set the brewery tone immediately and filled each tap with Indiana-only beers, including some from his friends at Lafayette Brewing. "When the brewery opens it's going to be no holds barred," he told us shortly after receiving federal approval for the brewery and ordering the necessary equipment. "If we're going to call ourselves craftsmen, we need to embrace that."

Months before he poured the first Black Swan Brewpub beers, McAllister had already set the bar high. First, all eighteen taps (including two beer engines for hand-pulled pints) will be pouring house-made beers. Second, he is going away from the trend that many have in offering generic recipes. He plans on crafting double IPAs, cream stouts, English-style bitters, and even dabbling in Belgian-inspired beers, like a sour Flemish Red. "Inevitably, some will not work," he said. "But to the extent that I have a brewery, I am going to have a lot of fun with it."

Black Swan Brewpub

Year Opened: 2010
Owners: D. J. and Erin McCallister
Brewer: D. J. McCallister
System: Custom
Production: 800 barrels estimated
Hours: Sunday, Tuesday through Thursday 11 A.M. to 10 P.M.; Friday and Saturday, 11 A.M.to midnight. Closed Monday.
Tours: Yes, on request when the brewer/owner is available
Take-out beer: Growlers
Extras: Outdoor seating with occasional live music
Special considerations: Family friendly, kids welcome, handicap accessible
Parking: On-site parking

Three Pints Brewing

 THREE PINTS BREWING   5020 Cambridge Way, Plainfield, IN 46168
www.threepintsbrewpub.com/
(317) 839-1000

Making beer and troubleshooting a nuclear submarine have some things in common, says Tom Hynes, who knows a little about both. Hynes owns Three Pints in Plainfield, a western suburb of Indianapolis. His brewpub is one of the state's newest.

"It's something I've dreamed about doing for a long time," Hynes, 50, said of the transition from sub to brewpub, where the global implications of tubes and knobs are different but the physics are the same.

Hynes is an Indianapolis native and has lived in Plainfield for years. Before opening Three Pints, he spent six years in the Navy, troubleshooting the nuclear reactor aboard the submarine USS *Ulysses S. Grant*. Now he's on the hunt for Red Oktoberfest.

The name Three Pints is partly in homage to a pub called Three Tons that Hynes frequented when he was stationed in London. It's also a reference to his three children, now all grown, who he called "half-pints" when they were little.

Three Pints will showcase a few of the best pours from Hynes's more than two decades as a homebrewer. One flagship beer will be a California common beer similar to Anchor Steam but with a tad less hops and a maltier, more biscuit-like flavor. Another featured brew will be a porter with a little oatmeal and finishing hops for flavor and aroma. "I'm very excited about that one," Hynes said.

Other brews will include an amber ale and an IPA. Three Pints will start off with four in-house brews, hopefully expanding to five within the first year, Hynes said. He will augment his own brews with taps featuring a few other Indiana-brewed beers.

The food is traditional American cuisine, including nachos, wings, pizza, jalapeño chips, tenderloin sandwiches, salads, and entrees, including a "rattlesnake pasta" with jalapeños and sausage. It also has a few vegetarian options and, of course, sub sandwiches.

In addition to his years spent homebrewing, Hynes also attended Chicago's Siebel Institute and spent a week working at the Green Bay Brewing Company in Wisconsin, which uses the same Criveller brewing equipment as Three Pints.

After his stint in the Navy was done in 1987, Hynes worked for the next two decades as a computer programmer. He said he thought about trying to open a brewpub in the mid 1990s, but didn't have the resources. The impetus to try now was the fact that his three kids have left home, leaving Hynes and his wife, Pam, time to plot their next undertaking. "We became empty nesters last year and craft beers are starting to resurge," he said. "So we thought, 'Now is the time.'"

While Three Pints opened in late November 2010 and is still so new as to not have a distinct niche yet, Hynes notes that it features seventy-five seats for family dining and contains eleven TVs. It does a brisk business on game days.

"We seem to be having more success drawing people when the Colts play than the Colts have at winning," Hynes joked during an unusually rough stretch for the hometown team.

Three Pints Brewing

Opened: 2011
Owner: Tom Hynes
Brewer: Tom Hynes

System: Four serving tanks, 5-barrel brewing system, one 10-barrel fermenter, one 10-barrel bright tank.

Production: 600 barrels (projected for 2011)

Tours: Yes, by appointment

Take-out beer: Growlers

Food: Full menu

Hours: Tuesday through Thursday, 4 P.M. to 11 P.M.; Friday, 4 P.M. to 12:30 A.M.; Saturday 11 A.M. to 12:30 A.M.; Sunday 11 A.M. to 11 P.M. Closed Mondays.

Parking: On-site lot

Heorot

219 South Walnut Street, Muncie, IN 47305
(765) 287-0173

The gentleman depicted with the two dogs on the side of Upland Brewing Company's six-packs of Ard Ri Imperial Irish-Style Red Ale is Muncie's Stan Stephens, owner of the Heorot and now one of Indiana's newest brewers. Stephens, who opened the Heorot in the mid 1990s specifically for beer lovers, was as of this writing installing an 11-gallon barrel for brewing on his building's third floor.

"I'm the one who has to carry the grain up there," he said. "So I guarantee we're not going to do hundreds of barrels a year."

Stephens said he plans to brew beer only for patrons who for years have bellied up to the bar in Heorot's narrow confines for a taste of the more than twenty craft beers they have on tap.

One of those customers was Caleb Staton, today the head brewer at Upland. This is how Stephens and his two wolf-hybrids, Harley and Wolfey, ended up on the six-pack holder for Ard Ri.

Stephens said he dreamed of making his own beer in Heorot ever since it opened. In the late 1990s he took a road trip through California with his friend Bob Cox, stopping at every brewery they could. Today Cox is the head brewer at Heorot, sharing the duties with Stephens.

Stephens said that Cox prefers hoppier beers while he prefers maltier ones, so they will likely brew both IPAs and stouts with some common ground in Belgian ales.

"I've been drinking great beer for so long," said Stephens, a Muncie native and part-time teacher. "This was just the next logical step."

Brewing Beer

At its most basic, beer consists of just four ingredients: water, grain, hops, and yeast. It is how those four are mixed, tinkered with, and fermented, however, that can be the difference between a great brew and one not even suitable to water plants.

When you visit the breweries mentioned in this book you'll see a lot of equipment of varying sizes. Most of it will be made of stainless steel and full of beer in some stage of the brewing process.

So, how is beer made? It starts out with the grain. Depending on the recipe or style, a variety of grains can be used. The whole grains are put through a gristmill in which they are cracked and opened. From there, the kernels are transported to the mash tun, where they are mixed with 155-degree water, where it steeps for a while. During this process, the sugars that will later turn this mixture into alcohol are broken down, leaving a thick oatmeal-like substance called *wort*. The wort is drained from the mash tun and transferred into a brewkettle.

By the way, according to industry statistics, most of the barley malt grown in the country goes to feed livestock. Only a small portion goes toward brewing. With this in mind, many breweries donate their spent grain to local farmers to be used as feed. Lucky animals!

Once the wort is in the brewkettle, it is brought to a boil. Hops, tiny cone-shaped vegetation that contain lupulin and give the beer a bitter or floral taste depending on the variety, are added at different intervals. Most boils last about ninety minutes but can go for less or more time depending on the recipe. Different hop varieties can be used, and the timing in the process for adding them will affect the end result. Brewers have a lot of fun experimenting during this step.

After the boil, the brew is brought through a heat exchanger that cools down the wort, and the liquid is emptied into a fermentation tank. It's at this point that the brewer's yeast is added. There are thousands of strains of yeast, and depending on the style of beer, a different strain can be added for the desired result. The yeast feasts upon the sugars in the wort, creating alcohol and carbon dioxide. This is where we finally get the beer.

But the process is not over yet. While some brewers will use fermentation tanks for aging, others will use bright beer or conditioning tanks where the beer can mature and strengthen for weeks, months, or even a year.

Before the beer is transferred to serving tanks, it is usually filtered. This step is skipped for some beers, such as wheats, because the haze is part of the allure and style of those brews. Other beers, like pale ale, should be clear.

Once in the serving tanks, the fun really begins. The tanks are connected to the taps behind a bar, or used to fill kegs, growlers, bottles, cans, or any other vessel one would use to transport beer.

This is, of course, a simplified version of how to make beer. The process can vary from brewery to brewery. Some places, because of space constraints or lack of equipment, will use malt extract, skipping the milling process. And the four ingredients that we mentioned are not the only things that one can put in beer. Virtually anything edible or drinkable can be added to a brew. Again, some work better than others.

Some breweries try to keep it pure by following the *Reinheitsgebot*, or the German Beer Purity Law, a nearly five-hundred-year-old regulation that originated in Bavaria and once dictated that beer may be made only with water, barley, and hops.

The bottom line is that the majority of beers being produced in the United States by craft brewers are of exceptional quality. Most brewers have gone through formal training and likely have an extensive home-brewing background. Like chefs, they experiment and try to find a recipe that will play well in their area. That's why an IPA made in Washington State will vary from one produced in New Jersey.

Taste accounts for something. We've been to brewpubs and breweries where people will have wildly different reactions to the same beer. In reality, both are right. No one knows your tastes better than you.

If you want to learn more about the brewing process or brewing at home there are a variety of resources that can teach you how to do it. Vendors sell equipment that range from filling a garage or simply taking up a corner in an apartment closet.

Should you choose to go that route, you'll experience a great sense of pride and accomplishment and a better understanding of the fermented beverage in your glass. And, you'll have something to talk about with the brewer at your local establishment next time you visit.

Crossroads of America
Indianapolis

For years, Indianapolis bore the stigma of nicknames like "Nap Town" and "Indiana-No-Place." But in the 1990s, construction and development downtown seemed to awaken the city, and today, a thriving cultural scene mixes with Hoosier hospitality and charm.

Indianapolis calls itself the "Crossroads of America," and rightly so. Four major interstates go through Indianapolis, connecting it to the major cities in each geographical direction—Chicago, Cincinnati, Louisville—and it has successfully established itself as a destination, not just a city on the way to someplace else.

As is the case with most major American cities, much of the focus for tourists in Indianapolis is downtown. It's anchored by the *Circle Centre Mall* and dotted with chain restaurants and nationally known stores. But peel away the retail layer, and the city begins to show its true colors.

When the weather cooperates, Indianapolis is a great walking city. The street grid was designed by an apprentice to Pierre L'Enfant, who designed Washington D.C., and in its center is a circle that connects the two main arteries: Meridian Street, which runs north to south, and Market Street, which runs east to west. The circle is home to the *Soldiers and Sailors Monument* (1 Monument Circle, 317-232-7615). Inside the base of the century-old, 284-foot-tall obelisk, you can look over the Civil War museum that chronicles the stories of Hoosier soldiers and then brave the 330 stairs (or take the elevator) to the top. It is the crown jewel of what is a downtown filled with historic monuments and architecture.

You can head west on the circle to see democracy in action at the *Indiana Statehouse*, the capitol building, or head north on Meridian Street where you'll encounter the past. Along North Meridian are several other grand monuments and feats of architecture, including the *Scottish Rite Cathedral* (650 North Meridian Street, 800-489-3579), which offers an hour-long guided tour. The neo-Gothic structure is believed to be the largest devoted to Freemasonry and is used as a meeting hall rather than as a house of worship. With its 212-foot tower, 54 bells, 2,500-pound gilded bronze chandelier, cavernous oak-paneled halls, and stained-glass windows depicting the thirty-three degrees of Freemasonry, the cathedral is a tribute to the organization's devotion to the arts, science, and religion. Just down the street is the *Indiana War Memorial*, a mausoleum-style building that rises 210 feet above street level.

There is a lot more than history to this city, and it has come a long way from an area that started out as a settlement for fur traders, but let's talk beer. The first brewpub opened in the early 1990s in Broad Ripple and was named for that neighborhood. Several more chain brewpubs opened their doors over the years, and they were followed by locally owned brewpubs. Sun King was the first commercial brewery to open in Indianapolis in about thirty years. There are a handful of breweries and brewpubs that were in various stages of opening when this book went to print in early 2011.

The beer bar scene has improved as well. At the early part of the last decade, people looking for a decent craft-brewed pint were hard-pressed to find one. Only a few places in town offered beers beyond those made by the mega-brewers like Budweiser and Coors. That too has changed, with many restaurants and bars now offering both local fare and delicious concoctions from celebrated breweries in Illinois, Michigan, and Colorado.

The change in beer culture probably developed as a result of Indianapolis beginning a sister-city relationship in 1988 with Cologne, Germany, the famous home of the golden-style ale known as Kölsch. Or, maybe it's because an intrepid few decided not just to pass through Indianapolis but set up shop and get down to brewing. Whatever the case, we can promise that you will find a locally made beer in this city that will make you want to stand up and shake the brewer's hand.

Music has played a big part in the writing of this book, and while cruising around town, we listened to a song by the Bottle Rockets called "Indianapolis." In it, the protagonist laments the fact that his van has broken down in the city, leaving him stuck for an undetermined amount of time. While we like the song, we couldn't agree less with the sentiments. Had our troubadour fully experienced Indianapolis and its local beer offerings, the song would have certainly come away with a different message. We hope that after a few days in the Circle City, you'll see why Indianapolis is not just a spot in the middle of going from one place to the other, but a city worthy of a closer look.

Lodging in the area: There is an abundance of chain hotels downtown that can accommodate just about every budget, but for a truly unique experience check into the Crowne Plaza, connected to the city's old Union Station. Twenty-six of its 273 rooms are in thirteen Pullman sleeping cars down on the track and are named for personalities from the early 1900s. 123 West Louisiana Street, 317-631-2221. Also check with the Indianapolis Convention and Visitors Association: www.visitindy.org.

Area attractions: Downtown has something for every age and for every type of personality. The *Indiana State Museum* (650 West Washington Street, 317-232-1637, www.indianamuseum.org) and the *NCAA Hall of Champions* (700 West Washington Street, 800-735-6222, www .ncaahallofchampions.org) are located in *White River State Park*, just a few blocks west of the circle. *The Children's Museum of Indianapolis* (3000 North Meridian Street, 317-334-3322, www.childrens museum.org) is one of the largest in the world and offers hours of interactive and educational fun.

For some old-time bowling fun, check out *Action Duckpin Bowl* and *Atomic Bowl Duckpin* (1105 Prospect Street, 317-686-6006). The hometown NFL team, the Indianapolis Colts, play at *Lucas Oil Stadium* (500 South Capitol Avenue, 317-262-8600, www.lucasoilstadium .com), which is home to Super Bowl XLVI in 2012. The NBA's Pacers play on the other side of downtown at the *Conseco Fieldhouse* (125 South Pennsylvania Street, 317-955-8271, www.consecofieldhouse .com); the arena's current craft beer offerings were severely lacking. So, thank goodness for baseball. Indiana does not have a major league team, so many Hoosiers will root for either the Cubs or the Reds. Indianapolis, however, is home to a minor league team, the Indians. The team plays at *Victory Field* (501 West Maryland Street, 317-269-3545), and over the last few seasons has partnered with local breweries, like Sun King, to offer good beer during the game. No visit to Indianapolis would be complete without a trip to the *Indianapolis Motor Speedway* (4790 West 16th Street, 317-492-6784, www.indianapolismotor-speedway.com). The *Hall of Fame Museum* within the racetrack grounds houses vintage racecars, trophies, and more than two dozen cars that actually won the Indy 500, including Ray Harroun's Marmon Wasp, which finished first in the race's inaugural running in 1911. The narrated bus ride around the fabled 2^1/$_2$-mile oval may be the closest you ever come to racing in the old Brickyard, but unfortunately the driver never gets above 30 miles an hour. The tour offers an up-close look at the famed racing pagoda, Gasoline Alley, and the last remaining strip of the track's original brick surface, 36 inches wide, which now serves as the start/finish line. If you're feeling athletic, rent a bike or some skates and take the **Monon Trail** (www.indianatrails.org/ Monon_Indy.htm) from the downtown **Mass Ave Arts District** to the fun and lively village of Broad Ripple. The trail runs past both Brugge Brasserie and the Broad Ripple Brewpub.

Other beer sites: While Indianapolis offers quite a few brewpubs and microbreweries, there are a few places we recommend that have either a good selection of microbrews or offer an experience like no other. **The Rathskeller** (401 E. Michigan St., 317-636-0396, www .rathskeller.com) is about as authentic a German biergarten you can get outside of Bavaria. Located in the Mass Ave Arts District down-town, the Rathskeller has won nearly every drinking and dining award from just about every publication in the state. It has been around since 1894 and has a good selection of rotating taps (available by the liter) and bottles from craft brewers and German breweries alike. During the warmer months the outside beer garden is a great place to gather with friends to enjoy sweeping views of the downtown skyscrapers. But with so many different rooms, each as welcoming as the next, the Rathskeller is a good bet any time of year.

For 109 years at **St. Elmo Steak House** (127 South Illinois Street, 317-635-0636, www.stelmos.com), patrons have sidled up for martinis, single malts, and a few rotating craft beers to the tiger oak bar, first used in the 1893 World's Columbian Exposition in Chicago. Settle in under the gaze of the Indiana celebrities, such as David Letterman and Larry Bird, whose photos adorn the walls, and try their not-for-the-faint-of-heart signature dish, the shrimp cocktail. The jumbo shrimp are served smothered in horseradish cocktail sauce made every hour to ensure freshness and a proper sinus assault. If you can see through the tears in your eyes, you'll probably notice one of the tuxedoed bar-tenders having a quiet chuckle at your expense.

Plump's Last Shot (6416 Cornell Avenue, 317-257-5867) is a comfy watering hole that opened in 1990. The swish at the climax of the 1986 film *Hoosiers* depicted the actual shot Bobby Plump sank on March 20, 1954, that pushed tiny Milan past goliath Muncie for the state title. Plump's Last Shot is a veritable museum of that season. The oak walls are adorned with the Converse All-Stars that Plump wore, the rope-basket through which he sunk shots, and classic photos of Indiana basketball stars. In the summertime, the outside porch is packed with revelers. The man himself is a frequent visitor, graciously conversing with both the reverential who pay homage to him and the oblivious who pay homage to the dozen bottles and three taps featuring revolving casks of craft beer from around the country. "I've lived a charmed life," Plump beams, surrounded by mementos of his career. "We didn't know what that shot meant at the time, we were just having fun."

Vollrath (118 East Palmer Street, 317-632-5199, www.vollrath indy.com) was built in 1926 on the south side of downtown. It is notorious for its alleged underground tunnels, which allowed infamous gangster and Vollrath regular John Dillinger to escape police. Featuring red walls and red lights, the cavernous space showcases some of Indianapolis's burgeoning musical talent on a stage out in front of the bar. Today, the Harley-riding barmaid slings bottles of Upland brews and Three Floyds' Gumballhead over the brass bar with wood trim. The locals are as colorful as the original stained-glass Vollrath sign that still hangs above the front door.

Red Key Tavern (5170 North College Avenue, 317-283-4601) is a bar with rules. Follow them or get thrown out of this quirky old tavern with charm and unique owners. Don't say we didn't warn you. *The Melody Inn* (3826 North Illinois Street, 317-923-4885) has live music, great bartenders, and local taps that make this near-dive bar one of our favorites. *MacNiven's Restaurant and Bar* (339 Massachusetts Avenue, 317-632-7268) is a Scottish pub with hearty food, a great whiskey selection, and a rotating selection of local beers.

Indianapolis is about the last place you'd expect to find it, but *Yats Cajun Creole Restaurant* (www.yatscajuncreole.com), with authentic New Orleans cuisine. has four locations around the city. From dirty rice and jambalaya to etouffee and gumbo, this place will cure what ails ya. Big, sloppy plates filled with spicy, flavorful goodness. Another good option is *John's Famous Stew* (1146 Kentucky Avenue, 317-636-621, indysfamousstew.com), which has been serving up hearty bowls for a hundred years. Get it with the butter beans and you won't be disappointed.

Tomlinson Tap Room (222 East Market Street, Indianapolis, www.indycm.com) is located inside the Indianapolis City Market. It opened in late 2010 and features nothing but Hoosier-made beer. The taproom features regular brewery events and offers growler fills.

Alcatraz Brewing Company

Circle Centre Mall, 49 W. Maryland Street, Suite 104
Indianapolis, IN 46204
(317) 488-1230 • www.alcatrazbrewing.com

Despite its name, Alcatraz Brewing Company in downtown Indianapolis is far from being an island. There is a Ram Brewery directly across the street and a Rock Bottom one block north. But, the quality ales and lagers that flow from the Alcatraz taps are what separate it from its fellow corporate-owned counterparts. There were other Alcatraz restaurants—owned by the Tavistock Restaurant Group—but these days Indianapolis has just one other sister site in Orange, California.

The crowd at Alcatraz is unquestionably tourist. With its proximity to a dozen or so downtown hotels, it's a gathering spot for the visiting crowd. Its interior, with a laminate bar and an open kitchen complete with a wood-fired pizza oven to the side, is typical, giving even weary travelers a place that looks familiar. The bar has a friendly staff that makes it feel like maybe the road isn't so hard.

The beers help as well. The friendly, talented, and accommodating brewers have earned a reputation for serving easy-drinking session beers, something some brewers have forgotten in an age of "extreme beers." Take a look at the colorfully illustrated chalkboard behind the bar and pick your poison. You really won't make a bad choice. When we visited then-brewer Omar Castrellon (who has since moved to 3 WiseMen), he was slightly disappointed in a cherry stout that he made with fifty pounds of fruit, but discovered the roasted malts hid the flavor. Next time, he said with a smile, he would just add more fruit.

The Pick: The Rock Bock has a nice touch of Mount Hood hops. This copper-colored German-style spring beer has a powerful malt mouth feel with a light and sweet finish.

In that statement he perfectly illustrated the tenacity of craft brewers. If you don't get it how you want it the first time, you keep trying. People will likely enjoy the efforts in the meantime and then appreciate it when it hits that perfect note.

The brewpub is in close proximity to the stadiums for the Colts and Pacers, and many sports fans

Beers brewed: Searchlight, Weiss Guy Wheat, India Brown Lager, Pelican Pale Ale, The Rock Bock, Cherry Stout.

use it as a pre-game or post-game stop. It's also particularly busy during racing season and when college basketball heats up every March.

Of course there are shoppers from the Circle Centre Mall who lumber in heavy with shopping bags (the brewery has its own mall entrance) for a quick bite and quaff. But more often than not, the brewery serves mostly anonymous business travelers who come and go like the tide. For those who feel that travel is like a prison sentence, this Alcatraz is not a bad place to spend behind bars.

Note: Alcatraz's corporate owner recently sold the restaurant's space to national chain California Pizza Kitchen. It was unclear at the time of this writing if the newcomers would keep the brewery equipment in place.

Alcatraz Brewing Company

Opened: 1995
Owner: Tavistock Restaurants
Brewer: Skip Duvall
System: 15-barrel Canadian BME system
Production: 400 barrels estimated for 2010
Brewpub hours: Monday through Thursday, 11 A.M. to 11 P.M.; Friday through Saturday, 11 A.M. to midnight; Sunday, noon to 9 P.M.
Take-out beer: Growlers
Food: Wood-fired pizza, burgers, generous dinner salads, and a lot of seafood dishes.
Special considerations: Handicapped-accessible
Parking: Circle Centre Mall has a parking garage across the street. Metered parking on the street.

Ram Restaurant & Brewery

140 South Illinois Street, Indianapolis, IN 46225
(317) 955-9900 • www.theram.com

Consistency is the name of the game here. No matter the day, no matter the season, beer drinkers at Ram are guaranteed consistent pints of blonde, hefeweizen, pale ale, porter, amber ale, and red IPA.

How serious is the company? So serious that they send their beers to a laboratory every two months to make sure every drop at

Sun King Brewery

135 N. College Avenue, Indianapolis, IN 46202
(317) 602-3702 • www.sunkingbrewing.com

Dave Colt and Clay Robinson were tired of polishing copper. As the brewer and assistant brewer, respectively, at Ram Brewery in downtown Indianapolis, one of their duties included polishing a copper cover for the brew tanks to give it a more aesthetic look.

Dave had worked at Ram since its opening in the early 2000s and Clay arrived a short time later. The two followed recipes as dictated by the company, but kept saying to each other that they should open their own brewery. The final straw came while they were on their knees one afternoon, cleaning products in hand. "I said, 'dammit, I think we can do it better with our own place,'" Colt remembered.

So, Clay left Ram in July 2008 to write the business plan for the pair's future brewery, and Dave stayed behind until it was finally time to open Sun King, the first nonchain microbrewery to open in Indianapolis in nearly three decades.

The name was Dave's idea. The brewery crew had been talking about a few names, trying to come up with one that would play well with seasonal beers, something that can be hard to come by in Indiana. At first they were leaning toward Solstice, until they discovered that a long-defunct brewery had claimed the name, making it unavailable.

Then Dave got to thinking about the earth and how the sun was responsible for all life on the planet. "I said, it's like the sun is our king," recalled Dave. "The name just came from there." A local artist who designed the brewery's tongue-bearing god for the logo borrowed heavily from the Aztec and Mayan calendars to depict seasonality.

The equipment came from an old system used by Stone Coast Brewing, and the men set up shop in an old dairy plant a few blocks from the center of downtown. It's a totally unremarkable building. It's brick and white aluminum siding on the outside, and it's located next to an armored car service.

The Pick: Cream ale gets a bad rap because it is associated with lesser breweries, but Sun King has brought honor back to the style with the Sunlight Cream Ale. It's deliciously smooth, with a heavy malt taste and nice hop background, and it's perfect for any time of year.

Beers brewed: Sunlight Cream Ale, Wee Mac Scottish Ale, Bitter Druid ESB Osiris Pale Ale, and a seemingly unlimited number of seasonal beers and one-offs.

Inside, however, is where the magic happens.

Realizing that there was no sense in waiting, Dave, who does most of the brewing, immediately got down to business. There are four year-round offerings: Wee Mac Scottish Ale, Sunlight Cream Ale, Osiris Pale Ale, and Bitter Druid ESB. They quite a few seasonal beers on the rotation, including an Octoberfest, a barley wine, a crab apple brew and one that they call El Gallo Negro.

Clay handles the sales and marketing end of things. While other upstarts might take it slow, test the market, and gauge customer reaction, Clay and Dave decided to put the hammer down and go for it. Within months of opening they purchased additional brewing equipment and installed a canning line.

While some may think that canning beer is a step down in the brewing world, many craft brewers are beginning to embrace the aluminum cylinders that allow consumers to easily take the good stuff where it's needed. It's both economical and better for the environment to use cans, say brewers. Unlike glass bottles, light can't penetrate cans, which helps against altering the intended taste. Sometimes known as "skunked beer," it's the result of light reacting with the hops and negatively changing the flavor profile. Sun King is canning three beers already in a 16-ounce size and plans to introduce more down the line.

These days their beer is available on tap at most of the better beer bars in Indianapolis, and on the weekends, people line up at the brewery for growler fills and the chance to sneak a taste of one of the many experimental brews they are constantly developing.

We had a fun few days hanging out at the brewery, which attracts folks from all walks of life. During hours that the tasting room is open, attorneys are hanging out with the artistic types, while computer-minded people clink glasses with chefs and writers. That's proof that good beer can always bring people together on common ground.

Less than nine months after brewing their first batch, the brewery collected two awards at the World Beer Cup, considered to be one of the more prestigious brewing competitions. For a relative newcomer to the local scene, we have very little doubt that Sun King will soon be a nationally recognized brand.

Sun King Brewery

Opened: 2009
Owners: Clay Robinson, Dave Colt, Omar Robinson, Andy Fagg, and Steve Koers.
Brewers: Dave Colt, Clay Robinson

System: 15-barrel JV North West Brewhouse

Production: 4,000 barrels estimated for 2010.

Tours: Thursdays and Saturdays by appointment. Tasting Room is open Thursday, 4 P.M. to 7 P.M.; Friday, 1 P.M. to 7 P.M.; Saturday, 1 P.M. to 4 P.M.

Take-out beer: 32-ounce and 64-ounce growlers, cans, 5.3-gallon and 15.5-gallon kegs.

Special considerations: Handicapped-accessible

Parking: Parking in front

Broad Ripple Brewpub

840 East 65th Street, Indianapolis, IN 46220
(317) 253-2739 • www.broadripplebrewpub.com

Should a patron walk into the Broad Ripple Brewpub and be reminded of an English pub because of its cozy dark-wood interior, beer memorabilia lining the walls, and even a Middleborough Football Club sticker on the mirror behind the taps, he or she could be forgiven.

Broad Ripple was founded by John Hill, an Englishman who hails from Middleborough. Hill and his wife had owned a wine bar in town and were inspired to open a brewery after a trip to California in the late 1980s when the country's microbrewing scene was beginning to blossom. According to manager Kurt Danenman,

"When they got back here they had the idea in their head and decided, 'Why don't we try it here?' And it just worked out."

Broad Ripple, built on the site of a former Napa Auto Parts store, prides itself on a laid-back attitude and a cast of regulars that lends character to the establishment. Many of the employees have worked there close to two decades, a testament to the lifestyle it facilitates.

"I just think we're one of the more comfortable places, we're broken in, we have a little bit of a laid-back attitude," Kurt said. "We like experiment-

The Pick: Some days you just want a light beer. It may be hot weather or just because your tastebuds are shot after a few rounds of IPA. The Lawnmower Pale Ale is perfect for those occasions.

Beers brewed: IPA, ESB, Extra Pale Ale, Lawnmower Pale Ale, Wobbly Wheat, Red Bird Mild, Java Stout, Hopsicle.

ing with food and with beer. Sometimes we'll get the wrong hops and instead of returning them, we'll use them."

The beers are courtesy of Kevin Matalucci, head brewer at Broad Ripple since 1993, who had been a carpenter before being hired. "We figured if he could build a garage, he could brew beers," Kurt said. "All you have to do is follow the notes and run the hoses, you can get fancy later." Kevin did exactly that, attending the two different brewing programs at the Siebel Institute in Chicago.

Kevin's philosophy is simple: Brew beers that people can enjoy and prolong their time out. "I'm a firm believer in the five-percent beer," Kevin said, referring to alcohol content. "I like to be able to go out and have several of them and not get too banged up." He added that in the brewing world there is a movement that favors "extreme beers," with alcohol contents up to and above 10 percent.

"When I go out with friends I like to be out for a while and you're not doing me any favors with the extra alcohol," he said. "I like a good drinking session."

Broad Ripple regularly features an IPA, Java Stout, a wheat beer, a light brew called Lawnmower, a hoppy brew appropriately titled Hopsicle, and an Extra Special Bitter. It also features cask ales, including a Monon Porter and a Wee Alec Heavy.

Notable at the Broad Ripple is the easy conversation. Whether the topic is sports, music, or the subject of the newest column in the *Indianapolis Star*, the chit-chat flows almost as easy as its fizzy facilitator. "The thing that keeps me coming back is the conversation," said Broad Ripple veteran and teacher Matt McMichael.

The brewery has only one TV, and because of the roots of the establishment's owner, when patrons ask what game is on, the answer is often an international soccer game.

Underneath a pressed tin ceiling, the elbow-shaped bar is tight. Around the perimeter of the room, which features a dining area and small room for playing darts, sit growlers, pint glasses, and steins from around the world. Most of them are gifts, said a comely, blonde, tattooed bartender who spoke of riding her bicycle around Indianapolis.

The menu features traditional English pub food—beef and potato dishes—with an American twist. The bar serves a modest yet scrumptious bison burger raised on a nearby ranch owned by a doctor who is a regular patron. While Broad Ripple serves growlers, it does not bottle its beer, frustrating some patrons but keeping them loyal customers.

The brewing room sits behind stained glass windows that feature the brewery name in plain sight from the bar. Brewer Kevin Matalucci likens working in there to "being in a fishbowl."

His product speaks for itself. John Sheehan, a surgical technician who lives in Indianapolis said there is one reason he keeps coming back. "There are some kick-ass beers here."

Broad Ripple Brewpub

Opened: 1990

Owners: John and Nancy Hill

Brewer: Kevin Matalucci

System: 7-barrel system from Wildcat Brewing Company, four fermenters.

Production: 1,000 barrels in 2009, 1,000 barrels estimated for 2010.

Brewpub hours: Monday through Thursday, 11 A.M. to midnight; Friday and Saturday, 11 A.M. to 1 P.M.; Sunday, noon to 10 P.M. (kitchen closes one hour before closing.)

Take out: Growlers

Tours: None, but picture windows allow full views of the brewery.

Food: English pub fare with vegan and gluten-free options.

Extras: On Monday, 20-ounce pints sell for $3; Tuesday is quiz night.

Special consideration: Handicapped-accessible

Rock Bottom Restaurant & Brewery

DOWNTOWN

10 West Washington Street
Indianapolis, IN 46204
(317) 681-8180 • www.rockbottom.com

People say hitting rock bottom is a bad thing. Nothing you'd want to repeat.

But in Indianapolis, jump at the chance to hit Rock Bottom. It's one of the city's best-known breweries. And thanks to its two locations, you can hit Rock Bottom twice, but never taste a repeat beer. Tim Fogleman, manager of the downtown location, explains the reason for that. "Our philosophy is each store has its own brewer and that's really important," he said. "A lot of national chains have to use the recipe that they're given, whereas we let our brewers have a lot of autonomy."

The Indianapolis Rock Bottoms share a similar beer template: the Circle City Light, Seasonal Wheat, Sugar Creek Pale Ale, Raccoon Red, Brickway Brown, Hoosier Ma Stout, and a few seasonal brews. Each one is not only brewed differently, but other factors such as local tastes and even different water supplies make beers of the same name different at each location.

The Pick: The Sugar Creek Pale Ale is a good introduction to the style. It has a pleasing taste with a nice hint of hops on the finish.

Beers brewed: Circle City Light, Sugar Creek Pale Ale, Raccoon Red, Brickway Brown, Hoosier Ma Stout.

Tim said that because the downtown Rock Bottom serves a wider cross section of the country— visitors who come for the city's numerous conventions and political and sporting events—the brewery strives to present as broad and varied a beer template as possible.

The menu here is loaded with classic American comfort foods. The grilled mahi sandwich is satisfying and the macaroni and cheese, baked with a little hot spice, is particularly good. On weekdays Rock Bottom packs out during lunchtime from all the office buildings in the area. In the summertime there is a pleasant outdoor dining area. One of the attractions is its proximity to the stately Soldiers' and Sailors' Monument, which is just a block away. The jewel of Indianapolis's downtown is flanked by fountains, surrounded by sculpture, and close to the city's other architectural treasures, including the Indiana Statehouse.

Brewer Jerry Sutherlin, a Greenwood native who speaks with a hint of a drawl, has brewed downtown for five years. His resume includes short stints at both Ram and Oaken Barrel. His favorite part of working at Rock Bottom is that his company's only rule is that the beers be fresh and unique. "It's somebody else's dime I get to have fun on," said Jerry, whose first order of business was to change the brewery's Raccoon Red from an Irish red to an ESB brewed with more English-style hops.

Jerry's product knocked out Arthur Corral, a forty-year-old FedEx employee from Las Vegas in town for a conference. "I drink a lot of IPA and by far that was the best one I had," he said.

Arthur's friend, thirty-four-year-old Matt Meyer, was particularly enamored of the brewery's location in relation to Ram and Alcatraz, also downtown. "Any place you can brewery hop is a good place," he said.

Rock Bottom Restaurant & Brewery—Downtown

Opened: 1994
Owner: Frank Day
Brewer: Jerry Sutherlin

System: 12-barrel JV Northwest Inc. system with four 24-barrel fermentation vessels

Production: 1,200 barrels in 2009; 1,200 estimated for 2010.

Brewpub hours: Sunday through Thursday, 11 A.M. to 1 A.M.; Friday and Saturday, 11 A.M. to 2 A.M.

Take-out beer: Kegs, pony kegs, growlers.

Tours: By appointment.

Food: Eclectic American menu, featuring Mexican and Asian dishes.

Extras: Occasional live music, pool tournaments, karaoke, Wii games, jukebox, and beer pong downstairs.

Special considerations: Handicapped-accessible.

Parking: Metered parking on street; garages nearby.

Rock Bottom Restaurant & Brewery

COLLEGE PARK

2801 Lake Circle Drive
Indianapolis, IN 46268
(317) 471-8840 • www.rockbottom.com

Clever country crooner Robbie Fulks sings, "Welcome to rock bottom, population one." Indianapolis, it could be said, is Rock Bottom, population two. The city's second Rock Bottom lies 15 miles north of the downtown location in College Park. While the name is the same, the beers are very different. The brewer too is pretty unique.

Liz Laughlin, who makes the suds at the College Park Rock Bottom, is as friendly as she is excellent at her job. "I get the best malt, I get the best hops, and everything you see here is 100 percent mine," she said. "All my own recipes."

Those recipes have scored Liz a grip of awards, including best in show at the Indiana State Fair in 2010 for her Simcoe IPA. She's won three gold medals and two best of shows in four years. In College Park, contrary to the myth that Midwesterners enjoy lagers, the hoppiest beers are the best sellers, said manager Matthew Kennedy.

"One wouldn't think that Indy is a hotbed for hop-heads, we're thought of a light beer-dominated market," he said. "But our biggest selling beer on tap at all times is the Double Barrel Pale Ale. Every time we have an IPA on tap we sell out in weeks if not nine or ten days."

Compared to the Downtown location, College Park is more spacious. The bar is horseshoe-shaped rather than straight. The walls are adorned with colorful vintage 1950s beer advertising, with a smiling couple enjoying a golden glass by a mountain lake in one and by the sea in another. Ceiling fans whir languidly. A big silo full of grain sits outside.

Sous-chef George Watson said he enjoys working with Liz to create food and beer pairings for the menu. Recently they collaborated on a pork chop with rosemary caramel sauce served with a cask of triple IPA. Another is a duck breast with apricot sauce combined with pints of seasonal wheat. "It's different than wine because I don't have to pair with a region," he said. "I coordinate with Liz, a person, and I enjoy the collaboration."

Originally from Cape Cod, Liz attended college in the hippie haven of Eugene, Oregon. She was lured, she said, by "school, brothers, and the outdoors." There she began homebrewing and over the years befriended local brewers. "I dove into it," she said. "It was my life."

She joined a homebrewing club, passed a beer judging certificate program, and her brews won local awards. Soon she was hired on at Steelhead Brewing Company in Eugene. That led to a job at Rock Bottom in Portland and eventually her transfer to Indianapolis in 2007.

During her tenure Liz watched the best-selling brew switch from the Circle City Light, which she said is "a Bud Light clone, not a beer for beer geeks," to the hoppier ales, signaling to her that her clientele has developed a more discerning palate for beers. "Now they want a more flavorful beer," she said. "We have a real hop-head following now, so I'm always going to have some kind of extra hoppy beer here."

That she's friendly is an extension of College Park's atmosphere, which Liz described as "handicapped friendly, kid friendly, gay friendly, politically friendly, you-name-it friendly."

Her smile is the only thing quicker than her wit. One of the few women in the country who brew professionally, she said, "Initially people were skeptical of my abilities. They said, 'You're not very big.' And then they taste the beer and they say, 'Oh, I like this.'"

Today, Liz Laughlin's signature adorns every growler sold at Rock Bottom in College Park. "I don't know why there aren't more women doing it," she said.

The Pick: We can't say enough good things about brewer Liz Laughlin. She knows how to get the most out of hoppy beers and for that we wholeheartedly endorse the Simcoe IPA. Hints of pine and citrus give this beer an earthy aroma. This is the kind of expertly made beer that will convert even the staunchest of hop adversaries to the style.

Beers brewed: Circle City Light, Double Barrel Pale Ale, Heartland Red, Hoosier Ma Stout, Brickway Brown, and many seasonal.

Rock Bottom Restaurant & Brewery—College Park

Opened: 2005
Owner: Frank Day
Brewer: Liz Laughlin
System: 12-barrel JV Northwest, Inc., system with five 24-barrel fermenters and eight 24-barrel servers.
Production: 950 barrels in 2009; 1,000 estimated for 2010.
Brewpub hours: Sunday through Thursday, 11 A.M. to 1 A.M.; Friday and Saturday, 11 A.M. to 2 A.M.
Take-out beer: Growlers
Tours: By appointment
Food: American
Extras: Karaoke on Thursdays
Special considerations: Handicapped-accessible
Parking: Free lot

Upland Tasting Room

4842 N. College Avenue, Indianapolis, IN
(317) 602-3931 • www.uplandbeer.com

Take a hip college-town coffee shop and replace the beans with hops and you've got the Upland Tasting Room. "Beerista" Sarah Fackler said the tasting room aims to turn tipplers on to new beer flavors.

"We wanted to let people know Upland has got a lot more to offer than just what's in the bars downtown," she said. Beers here come in "flights," five-ounce glasses that sell in threes and sixes (three flights is one ounce short of a pint).

This way, customers can taste an array of brews. "Upland opened this place with the intention that people experience their entire beer library," Sarah said. "Even teeny-tiny batches of beer are sent up here, even if they're not distributed through the rest of Indiana."

Doug Dayoff, president of Upland Brewing, says the tasting room has a tiny 1/2-barrel brewing system, so the beers brewed on location will be "more experimental than core, in essence a pilot system for our brew crew to try new recipes."

Beers brewed: Rotating seasonal and small test batches.

The arty ambiance reflects the room's brewing philosophy. The pea soup–green walls are adorned with funky, local artwork, including brown-painted tree limbs sprouting wilted vinyl record flowers, a guitar decorated with turquoise picks, and a tapestry made of neckties. None of the tables have matching chairs, but all are adorned with games such as Jenga, Scrabble, and Pictionary.

A comfortable sofa and armchairs sit atop throw rugs and soulful sounds waft over the stereo. There's enough light to read a textbook or leave a doodle in a scrapbook for visitors.

A bulletin board labeled "suggestions" displays sticky notes left by patrons. "Free Beer," reads one. "Boobies," reads another.

Upland Tasting Room

Opened: 2010
Owner: Doug Dayoff
Brewpub hours: Monday through Thursday, 2 P.M. to 10 P.M.; Friday and Saturday, 12 noon to 10 P.M.; Sunday, 12 noon to 8 P.M.
Take-out beer: Growlers
Parking: Street parking available.

Scotty's Thr3e Wise Men Brewing Company

1021 Broadripple Avenue
Indianapolis, IN 46220
(317) 255-5151
http://thr3ewisemen.com/

After more than a decade of running successful restaurants that proudly featured wide craft beer selections, it only made sense that Scott Wise would get into the brewing game himself.

In fact, when he opened his first restaurant (Scotty's Brewhouse in Bloomington) in 1996 he actually wanted to install a brewery. Good thing he didn't, he told us, because it likely wouldn't have ended in a positive way.

"I was very naive," he said. "Things worked out the right way."

Now, with six restaurants in his Indiana-centric empire, Wise realized it was time to get into brewing. When a space opened up on the site of a former grocery store, Scott saw the perfect location to make beer that will supply the other restaurants, room for a prep kitchen that will also serve the other restaurants in the family, and even space for a pizza kitchen.

What he opened was a very comfortable space with a lodge-type feeling: natural cedar planks on the walls, a high ceiling, exposed brick. There are custom-made picnic tables, each seating eight people, fostering a sense of community. The menu is simple, featuring pizza and burgers. That serves to highlight the beers and separate this location from the others in the Scotty's chain, which in some cases can have upwards of 150 items on the menu.

Beers Brewed: Two Lucy's Blackberry Wheat, Holdenzoe IPA, Centennial Martyr Double IPA, King Solomon's Imperial Stout, Naptown Nut Brown, Snow Bunny Blonde, Hubbards & Cravens Porter, Hoggy Style Amber.

Scott also wanted to make sure that he had a talented and passionate brewer at the helm of this new enterprise. He didn't have to look too far to find just the right person for the job: Omar Castrellon.

After stints in North Carolina, Alabama, and other states, Omar answered an ad in a local paper and flew to Indiana for a job interview at Alcatraz, where he spent the weekend cleaning tanks and brewing with his predecessor. He flew back home after the marathon session, and a few weeks later was rewarded with the job. He flew back to Indiana and has called it home ever since. When Wise announced he would be opening a brewery, he reached out to Omar for possible ideas on who he should hire. Turns out Omar was looking for a new challenge and the chance to be at a brewery from its beginning.

Of all the recently opened brewpubs in the state, this is among the most promising. With an experienced restaurateur and brewer combining forces, make sure you call ahead for reservations at a place that's likely to be regularly packed.

Scotty's Thr3e Wise Men Brewing Company

Opened: 2010
Owner: Scott Wise
Brewer: Omar Castrellon
System: 12-barrel premiere stainless system
Production: N/A
Brewpub hours: Monday through Thursday, 5 P.M. to midnight; Friday, 5 P.M. to 1 A.M.; Saturday, noon to 1 A.M.; Sunday, noon to 10 P.M.
Take-out beer: Growlers
Food: Pizza, burgers, etc.
Special considerations: Handicapped-accessible
Parking: Available lot

Triton Brewing Company

5764 Wheeler Road, Indianapolis, IN 46216
(317) 508-3715 • www.tritonbrewing.com

Though it lacks the storied history of Indiana brewing institutions like the Broad Ripple Brewpub in Indianapolis or Power House in Columbus, rookie Triton Brewing plans to waste no time establishing itself as one of the state's best.

"All guns blazing, we're bringing it," said cofounder Mike DeWesse. "We want to be an industry leader and we want to be a brewery Indiana can be proud of."

The idea for Triton took hold of DeWesse in 2002. At the time, he owned four Buffalo Wild Wings restaurant franchises and made sure they featured taps from Indy breweries like 3 Floyd's, Oaken Barrel, and Upland Brewing Company. To hear DeWesse tell it, he "was forcing good beer down the gullets of people as far away as Plainfield, Indiana, where they thought yellow beer was gospel."

DeWesse bought and sold more restaurant franchises in the ensuing years, each keeping with the theme of pushing Indiana-made beer. In 2003 he was elected to the board of the state's microbrewer's guild, a position he still holds in order to help "push as much Indiana beer as possible."

By 2009, DeWesse was working at Great Crescent Brewing Company in Aurora. DeWesse was also an early shareholder in 3 Floyd's; in 2007, he got a copy of 3 Floyd's business plan. He and partner David Waldman made a few tweaks to tailor the plan for their brainchild, Triton.

In March of 2010 they bought brewing equipment from the shuttered Warbird Brewing Company in Fort Wayne. At the time of this writing, they were looking for a space to start brewing, with an eye toward quickly building a tasting room.

But the most important piece for DeWesse was finding the person to run the brewing equipment. "I can sell ice to Eskimos," he says. "But I can't sell bad beer to anybody."

DeWesse's first move was to team with brewer Jon "Brewer" Lang, whose beers have medaled three times in four years in the Great American Beer Festival. The Minnesota native started homebrewing in 1990, and had brewed for nearly a decade at Barley

Beers brewed: Railsplitter IPA, Four-Barrel Brown Ale, Magnificent Amber Ale, Fieldhouse Wheat, Dead Eye Stout

Island, racking up a respectable number of awards. DeWesse offered to make him a partner at Triton, "to chain him to the tanks," as he says. Lang agreed.

Lang says his goals are to have five baseline beers on tap always, and release a new seasonal brew every two months. The constant beers will be a wheat, a brown ale, a stout, an IPA, and an amber ale.

Lang's method of brewing is to first perform reverse osmosis on the water, to strip it of all minerals. The he adds minerals back in to suit the water to each particular style of beer.

DeWesse said his goal is to make sure that each beer is "the most flavorful for its style." As he did when he invested in 3 Floyds, he's putting his money where his mouth is. Only this time, he's all in. "This is not a hobby," DeWesse said. "This is my retirement."

Triton Brewing Company

Opened: 2010

Owners: Michael C. Deweese, Jon W. Lang, and David M. Waldman

Brewer: Jon Lang

System: HDP (Heavy Duty Products) system from the old Warbird Brewing Company. The system is a 20bbl system capable of step mashing. Steam heated with a whirlpool.

Production: N/A

Tours: Call ahead for times

Take-out beer: Growlers available

Parking: On-site parking lot and handicapped accessible

Flat12 Bierwerks

414 North Dorman Street
Indianapolis, IN 46202
(317) 635-BEER • www.flat12.me

The first thing the owners of this brewery want you to know: the name is Flat, the beer is not. Flat12 Bierwerks, which is among the newest of the Indianapolis-based breweries, has ambitious goals to become a global brand, nearly as fast as its namesake.

Flat12, according to brewery co-founder Steve Hershberger, is a nod to the 12-cylinder internal-combustion engine that was once used in automobile racing. With Indianapolis's proud history in motor sports, the name made sense.

Hershberger told us that the brewery, which opened in late 2010, would be working around the clock to produce 12,000 barrels in its first full year of operation and would hit 30,000 within three years in its goal to become a global brand. "Our beers are very atypical," Hershberger said. "We zig when everyone else zags."

Indeed. Beers like the seasonal Glazed Ham Porter, brewed with "spices of a favorite holiday platter and the deep-roasted malt of the finest porter" will be available, according to the brewery.

That's just one porter we'll be seeing from Flat12. As the brewery's website makes clear, head brewer Rob Caputo "loves porters." It also adds, "He loves experimenting with herbs, spices, and other flavors. He doesn't like overt flavors and styles, preferring well-orchestrated subtlety."

The current brewing plan is to offer six year-round beers and two seasonals (the other being Flat Jack Pumpkin Ale). Flat12 also wanted to bring some social aspects to its brewery, so before it opened its doors and fired up the brewkettles it created an online community called Hopstars, which encourages people to share their beer-related thoughts and reviews on the brewery's website. Participants earn points, like a game, giving an incentive for many to return again and again.

"No one enjoys craft beer sitting in a basement by themselves," Hershberger said. "Virtually everyone enjoys the socialization of craft beer. We're helping with that through Hopstars."

Flat12 Bierwerks

Opened: Flat12 Bierwerks sold its first beer in November 2010 and officially opened its doors to the public in December 2010.

Owners: Rob Caputo, Sean O'Connor, Steve Hershberger

Brewers: Director of Brewing Operations, Rob Caputo; Brewer, Tom Block

System: 20bbl, three-vessel DME brewhouse with four 40bbl fermenters

2010 Production 2010: 500 barrels (reflects less than one month of 2010 production)

Tours: As part of private VIP events and tastings, the brewery offers a comprehensive tour of the facility, as well as of the brewing process. Scheduled public tours are also available.

Take-out beer: All year-round, specialty, seasonal, and premium beers are available for carryout in 64-ounce growlers. Certain beers are also available for carryout in six-pack sleeves.

Special considerations: Flat12's publicly accessible common areas are ADA compliant.

Parking: Flat12 has ample parking available at the brewery. Street parking is also available, as is an overflow lot for large events.

Hours: The brewery is open to the public during posted business hours Thursday through Sunday.

The Bier Brewery and Taproom

5133 East 65th Street, Indianapolis, IN 46220
http://www.bierbrewery.com/

Good things are destined to come in small packages at Bier Brewery, one of Indianapolis's newest breweries. It is run by Darren Connor, who for a decade sold homebrew equipment in the area.

The brewery will pump out five hundred growlers per week and the pours will include a pale, a Belgian blonde, a German wheat, a Kölsch, a brown, a porter, an oatmeal stout, a pumpkin ale, and other seasonal and experimental brews including IPAs, chocolate stouts, winter porters, and two different pale ales. "Ours will always be changing and it will be fresh, fresh, fresh," Connor said.

Connor, 33, said he started homebrewing in college at Indiana University because "when you can't buy it the next best thing is making it." He turned pro during a three-year stint at Bloomington Brewing Company. He went on to sell homebrewing equipment at Great Fermentations, which is only a few doors down from Bier Brewery in a light industrial neighborhood. He worked his way up to manager at Great Fermentations, and then three years ago began hatching a plan to open Bier Brewery.

"I thought it would be more fun to make it and sell it rather than just tell other people how to make it," he said. "When I set my mind to something, I usually get it done."

The vision for Bier Brewery was to keep it small, brewing just 40-gallon batches of any particular beer at a time, in order to keep the product dynamic. All Bier Brewery beer will either be quaffed in pint glasses in the tasting room or carried out in a growler. Connor said he has no, nor does he want any, outside accounts. "I don't want to be dictated," he said. "Too many commercial breweries get stuck in that rut."

As of this writing, the brewery is open on Fridays and Saturdays from 3 P.M. to 7 P.M. and on Sunday from noon to 4 P.M. Connor notes that the latter makes it a perfect stop before attending or hosting a football-watching party.

The rest of the week is dedicated to making beer. Connor cultivates eight different yeast strains and even customizes his water through reverse osmosis in order to get his optimal brewing ingredients. "It allows us to do whatever we want," he said.

The fact that he's so close to his former homebrewing employer was advantageous as well. He initially wanted to open in the South Broad Ripple neighborhood, but found rents there to be north of $15 a square foot. He found a warehouse three doors down from Great Fermentations for just $6 a square foot, big enough for 2,500 square feet of brewing space and a 1,500-square-foot tasting room.

The brewery celebrated a soft opening in late November 2010. Its website boasts that its utmost priority is creating beer that is "freaking awesome."

"We can brew whatever we want, that's the beauty of it," Connor said. "We're able to put out five hundred growlers a week, and then we're done until the next week."

The Bier Brewery and Taproom

Opened: November 2010

Owner: Darren Connor

Brewer: Darren Connor

System: Blitzen Engineering, four 50-gallon bright tanks, four 80-gallon bright tanks, 42-gallon fermenters.

Production: 500 barrels (projected)

Hours: Friday and Saturday, 3 P.M. to 7 P.M.; Sunday noon to 4 P.M.

Tours: Yes—consult website for times

Take-out beer: Growlers

The Hoosier State

Every state has a nickname. Some are more self-explanatory than others. With hundreds of miles of beaches, Florida calls itself the Sunshine State. This makes sense. South Dakota reminds people of its main attraction by calling itself the Mount Rushmore State. Other states focus on flowers (Mississippi is the Magnolia State), agriculture (Utah is the Beehive State), and animals (Oregon is the Beaver State) to define their identity. Still others emphasize their role in American history; Delaware, being the first to ratify the United States Constitution, appropriately calls itself the First State.

When it comes to nicknames, however, Indiana clearly wins the head-scratching competition with the nickname Hoosier State.

Residents identify themselves as Hoosiers. The Indiana University athletic teams use the name as well. Hoosier is on the license plates and every conceivable knickknack at the airport gift shop.

Ask a Hoosier to define the word or provide its etymology, however, and be prepared for a different story each time. We found it to be a great conversation starter and couldn't have been happier with the stories people shared.

Sherry, our bartender at Barley Island Brewing Company in Noblesville, relayed a story first told to her by her fourth-grade teacher. It's an old boxing term, for when a fighter would lose an ear and someone would pick up the detached lobe and ask "Whose ear?"

Improbable.

A legend, retold by Rock Bottom Downtown brewer Jerry Sutherlin, that many concede might actually be true, has a wealthy southern Indiana landowner by the name of Hoosier. His workers crossed the river to Kentucky to help the residents after a natural disaster. From that time, the neighbors to the north were all known by his name.

Ashley Herring, who also works at Rock Bottom Downtown, said Hoosier is short for "Who's there?" The image conjured is that of an ornery backwoodsman cocking a rifle to a stranger at his cabin door. Many other people tell this story.

Tom Stilabower of Indianapolis has a simple one. He said, "The definition of Hoosier is a Kentuckian on his way to Michigan when his car broke down."

Jim Herter, who works for *Great Lakes Brewing News* out of Granger, said he believes the name has to do with the leggings that early French settlers wore.

"All the French in the area would wear hosiery on their legs," he said. "It got slanged into Hoosier."

Mike Bachman, a school principal, said his father and uncles told him that a Hoosier is a chipmunk that runs across a golf green and disrupts a putt. Another definition Mike heard has to do with animals also.

"A husband and wife were talking intimately. The wife was trying to ask her husband something, but then an owl swooped down and said, 'Who,' right as he said 'sure.'" said. "Then they had dirty, dirty sex. I don't know any more of the story than that."

Over pints at the New Albanian Bank Street Brewhouse, Ed Needham, a member of the local homebrew club, raised his arms in mock exasperation and shook his head after he was asked about the word.

"There are twelve different definitions and none of them are right," he said.

Beth Howard, another member of the brewclub, chimed in, "Everyone has a definition just like every family has a fruitcake recipe, of you know, a relative who is a fruitcake."

A few weeks later, we were discussing it with *Indianapolis Star* reporter Jon Murray while at Brugge Brasserie. Some dude, walking past us and eavesdropping, said "It means redneck and I don't care because I am one!"

Bingo.

Jeffrey Graff of the Reference Department at the Herman B. Wells Library at Indiana University in Bloomington wrote, "Hoosier was a term of contempt and opprobrium common in the upland South and used to denote a rustic, a bumpkin, a countryman, a roughneck, a hick, or an awkward, uncouth, or unskilled fellow."

Few people use it that way anymore. And rightly so. Hoosier is a state of mind, a certain friendly attitude that one would best associate with a time when things were simpler. It's about teamwork and determination. It's about patriotism despite party lines.

The vast majority of Hoosiers that we've met are unfailingly polite, endlessly welcoming, and represent the core values that make this country what it is.

We might not understand the name, but it's a privilege to know the people.

More Than Just a College Town
Bloomington

It can be easy to think of Bloomington as just another college town. As home to Indiana University, it has close to 110,000 students, and the school colors—red and white—dominate just about every surface possible. But, spend some time in Bloomington and it will quickly reveal itself as an artistic and vibrant city that melds cultures and philosophies into a harmonious community.

Grand architecture, made by expert craftsmen, stands proudly on many of the streets near downtown. Trees of numerous varieties offer a nice canopy in the summer and a brilliant shower of foliage each autumn. One street in particular, Washington, comes immediately to mind as the kind of residential area that one would hope to find just off Main Street USA.

Downtown there are historic buildings, such as the ***Monroe County Courthouse***, which was constructed back in the days when civic buildings were designed as works of beauty, not just functional spaces. The courthouse and its grounds take up a city block, and most visitors will find themselves, after a minute of staring, asking what's with the fish? Atop the weathervane on the courthouse is a fish, telling passers-by which way the wind is blowing. According to the website for the Monroe County Library, the reason for the fish may have to do with the religious beliefs of a local blacksmith. Austin Seward made the weathervane for a courthouse constructed in 1827. That building was replaced in 1906 by the one standing today. "Mr. Seward was a Presbyterian church elder and probably chose the fish because of its Christian symbolism," writes the library on its website. "Also, fish were common on weathervanes in the eastern and southern parts of the country." So, now you know the answer when the person peering at the top of the building asks the fish question aloud in your presence.

Downtown is home to a great mix of restaurants, bars, shops, and galleries. It is easy to lose several hours taking a stroll and getting immersed in the various storefronts. If retail therapy is not your thing, the Bloomington area also has some great outdoor recreation options. One notable location is the *Charles C. Deam Wilderness Area*, 13,000 acres of the Hoosier National Forest. With trails for both novice and experienced hikers, it also has several camping areas. Or hit the water at Lake Monroe, the state's largest inland lake, where you can take advantage of all kinds of water sports and fishing. It's also a great place for bird-watching.

Now, we've said that Bloomington is more than a college town, and that's true. But it's tough to ignore *Indiana University* completely. Much of the IU that we know and love today is thanks to Herman B Wells, who spent most of his life associated with the school. As president from 1938 to 1962 and then as chancellor until his death in 2000, Wells is credited with turning the university into a world-class research facility. A bronze statue of his likeness was dedicated in 2000 and sits on a park bench, hand extended in a friendly greeting. IU is also a Big Ten school, home to the fighting Hoosiers, whose fans regularly pack the basketball arena and football stadium on game nights, with unwavering support.

Bloomington is one of those cities we love to come back to again and again. Visit and you'll see why.

Lodging in the area: Perhaps the most comfortable and friendly place to stay is the Showers Inn, a bed-and-breakfast housed in two lovingly restored twentieth-century homes. Well-appointed rooms with modern amenities, such as iPod docks, make this place feel like home. Don't miss the great hot breakfast served each morning in the formal dining room. We owe thanks to the owner, who dissuaded a traffic officer from giving us a ticket after we parked in a residents-only spot. You don't get treatment like that at most places. We'll be back. 430 North Washington Street, 812-334-9000, www.showersinn.com. There are several other options as well. Contact the Greater Bloomington Chamber of Commerce at www.chamberbloomington.org/cwt/external/wcpages/index.aspx.

Area attractions: If you're in the mood to for an adult beverage of a different variety, Bloomington is home to *Oliver Winery* (8024 N. State Road 37, 800-25-TASTE, www.oliverwinery.com), the largest in the state. Oliver has nice gardens for walking and a cheese shop. For some culture the *Indiana University Art Museum* (1133 East 7th Street, 812-

855-5445, www.artmuseum.iu.edu) has an impressive collection, including paintings by Picasso and Monet. Did you feel that rumble? You may want to check out the **Indiana Geological Society** (611 North Walnut Grove, 812-855-7636, www.igs.indiana.edu) and see its real-time seismic station in action. For a step back in time, visit the **Starlite Drive-in Theatre** (7640 Old State Road 37, 812-824-8036), which shows movies on the big screen outdoors.

Other beer sites: *Irish Lion Restaurant and Pub* (212 West Kirkwood Avenue, 812-336-9076, www.irishlion.com) is perhaps one of the best-known bars in town. Not the best craft selection, but people go for the sense of tradition and the atmosphere. *Scotty's Brewhouse* (302 North Walnut Street, 812-333-5151, www.scottysbrewhouse.com) is one of several in this state-wide chain. Good draft selection, huge portions of food, and a perfect example of an American sports bar. *Yogis Grill & Bar* (519 East 10th Street, 812-323-9644, www.yogis.com) has a draft collection that will make you smile. You'll be happy they have comfortable bar stools because you'll want to be there a while. *Crazy Horse Food and Drink Emporium* (214 West Kirkwood Avenue, 812-336-8877, www.crazyhorseindiana.com) is another local legend, with an impressive bottled beer selection and a chance to get your name on the wall if you drink "around the world."

No trip to Bloomington is complete without a stop at *Nick's English Hut* (423 East Kirkwood Avenue, 812-332-4040, www.nicksenglish-hut.com). Established in 1927, it is the quintessential college bar. It's also home to "Sink the Biz," a drinking game that involves about two pitchers of beer, a bucket, and a floating glass. We don't recommended playing this game with a Russian Imperial stout or double IPA, but if you're game, everyone should do it at least once. *Max's Place* (109 West 7th Street, 812-336-5169, www.maxsplace.info) has rotating taps and good pizza.

It happens to the best of us. An evening at the bar can suddenly turn into an all-nighter, especially in a college town. While you were quaffing those great beers, the kitchen closed, leaving you hungry on the way home. Bloomington has fast-food options and late-night pizza joints, but we nearly jumped for joy when we saw the *Insomnia Cookies truck* (www.insomniacookies.com, found along Kirkwood Avenue). Warm, chewy, and delicious fresh-baked cookies were a blissfully sweet way to end the night. Plus, they will deliver within a two-mile radius downtown.

Lennie's/Bloomington Brewing Company

1795 East 10th Street, Bloomington, IN 47408
(812) 323-2112 • www.bbcbloomington.com

The vision for Bloomington Brewing Company is that its mid-campus location will soon be a satellite to a much larger operation to the northwest of town, a sustainable farm where beer is brewed and water buffalo roam. For now, though, it's just a fine, local establishment in the middle of Indiana University's Bloomington campus, and a trend-setter in the state.

"This was the first small brewpub in southern Indiana," said David Schwandt, director of internal affairs, who for years has worked for owner Jeff Mease. Jeff started working in the location in 1982, when it was an eatery called Pizza Express. That transformed into a restaurant called Lennie's in 1989, which is still open and featured on the promi-nent sign adorning the building's roof.

The restaurant was named after Jeff's then-wife, Lennie Busch. Though the two have been divorced for nearly twenty years, they are still business partners and have a good personal relationship, David said. At the inception, there was talk of naming the brewery Busch Gardens II, a sly nod to the theme park once owned by the Anheuser-Busch company and keeping with the idea of naming establishments after Jeff's business partner and ex-wife. The idea was later scrapped.

In the early 1990s, after Jeff had spent much of the late '80s contemplating and planning a brewery, the Copy USA location next door to Lennie's became vacant. Jeff had thought about opening the brewery at another location, but opted to rent out the space next door and build his brewery inside.

"That's where the idea came from of expanding Lennie's into what it is today," David said.

The space is like a nifty campus eatery, featur-ing well-lit tables where co-eds can be seen snack-ing and reading thick textbooks. Local artwork adorns the walls.

The Pick: It's a rarity in the state, so your best bet is to go with whatever they are currently serving on nitrogen. It's the way Guinness is served in bars, the slow pour through the thin spout. The nitrogen forces the beer through the tap, giving it that creamy texture. Bloomington rotates their beers on the nitrogen, which adds a new layer of depth.

Beers brewed: Quarrymen Pale Ale, Freestone Blonde, Ruby Bloom Amber, Big Stone Stout, and a few sea-sonal beers.

Eileen Martin, who for nearly four years had brewed at neighboring Upland Brewery, is a recent addition to the Bloomington Brewing team. The architect of the Banshee Scotch Ale, which still draws raves at Upland, Eileen said that she plans to create more specialty beers in her new job at Bloomington. "I consider myself a chef of sorts in the beer industry," Eileen said. "I have a passion for it."

The brewery always has five beers on tap: a blonde, a ruby, a pale ale, a weiss, and in winter, a stout. There are also as many as two cask beers. Eileen works with the large, stainless-steel brewing tanks, visible through a window in a room just behind the elbow-shaped Indiana limestone bar. She described herself as a perfectionist. "I'm true to style when it comes to brewing," she said. "I make sure it falls in the proper color, malt, and hop parameters."

A native of Louisville, Kentucky, Eileen is a member of the Pink Boots Society, an organization founded by Oregonian Teri Fahrendorf and dedicated to promoting women who brew. Teri worked at Steelhead Brewing in Eugene, Oregon, along with Eileen's sister in suds, Liz Laughlin, now head brewer at the Rock Bottom College Park in Indianapolis. In homage to the society, Eileen literally wears pink boots while she brews. "I'm definitely in the minority," she said. "But there are more women brewing all the time."

The company will soon expand its brewing operation to a warehouse on the west side of town, which will allow brewing with a 20-barrel system rather than the 15-barrel system on campus. That will free up the campus location for specialty beers, such as cask ales, Eileen said. "It will allow us to make more specific beers here and give us a bigger distribution in general."

Jeff said the vision for the company is to soon expand to the 75-acre Loesch Road Farm, northwest of Bloomington. Already a few of the hops that the brewers use come from the farm, as do some of the vegetables served in the restaurant. The farm has around twenty pigs, which keeps the restaurant in fresh, smoked bacon.

The farm is also the only one in Indiana that raises domesticated Asian water buffalo. Jeff bought the buffalo after a European trip in which he learned about making one of his favorite cheeses, buffalo mozzarella. "My dream is to one day be able to serve customers a Caprese salad with Mozzarella di Bufala, cured salami, and a farmouse ale," Jeff said. "Every bit of it raised lovingly on this farm."

Jeff also dreams of his farm having a catering kitchen, a brewing and bottling facility, and a beer garden. "It's going to take some time," he said. "The best things do."

Lennie's/Bloomington Brewing Company

Year Opened: 1994
Owners: Jeff Mease, Lennie Busch
Brewers: Floyd Rosenbaum, Eileen Martin
System: 15-barrel Specific Mechanical and 20-barrel Premier Stainless.
Production: 900 barrels estimated for 2010.
Brewpub hours: Daily, 11 A.M. to midnight.
Take-out beer: Growlers, quarts
Food: Gourmet pizza, fabulous salads, and distinctive sandwiches. The brewery uses ingredients from local farmers and has a great wine list too.
Special considerations: Handicapped-accessible; children allowed in dining room. "Unattended children will be given espresso and a free puppy," according to Jeff.
Parking: Plenty of parking in a nearby lot.

Upland Brewing Co.

350 West 11th Street, Bloomington, IN 47404
(812) 336-BEER (2337) • www.uplandbeer.com

One of the great American pairings is a burger and beer. If it's a bison burger and a pint of one of Upland's brews, the culinary experience gets much better. On two separate occasions, we sat, ate, and took deep sips from our beer. Little conversation was shared—a sure sign of a good meal—although satisfied grunts escaped between bites.

On the fringe of the Indiana University campus, Upland Brewing occupies a large, squat building, with a restaurant in front and brewery in back. Opened in 1998, it's one of the oldest new-generation breweries in the state and is now among the most commonly found Hoosier brands throughout Indiana. Their Upland Wheat, a good representation of the style, also makes the occasional appearance in the background of the NBC show *Parks and Recreation*, based in the fictional town of Pawnee, Indiana.

Upland is a bit of a hybrid. It's a commercial brewery that has a restaurant attached, so it's probably incorrect to call it a brewpub. Besides, not many brewpubs make anything close to 6,500 barrels a year. Visitors can get a tour of the brewery on Saturday afternoons, so if you arrive at another time, the majority of what you'll be able to see through the large window behind the bar is an oak tank used to produce a wide line of lambics.

Lambic is a Belgian-style beer with fruit added. The name is derived from a small town southwest of Brussels. It is a most unique beer, because during fermentation it relies on wild yeast native to the area in Belgium. Lambics can be slightly sour, with little evidence of hops and, depending on what is added, can give a nice fruit kick without being soda sweet. Raspberry is usually the most common lambic, but the brewer at Upland, Caleb Stanton, is not afraid to get unusual. In the last few years he has released persimmon, peach, kiwi, and strawberry versions of lambic. Each is aged for about a year in old white-wine oak barrels before the whole fruit is added. It's bottled in a size suitable for sharing.

Caleb has an impressive and wildly varying array of beers from the wheat to an Imperial IPA. He always seems to be experimenting as well, so you never quite know what you'll find on tap at your next visit.

Bloomington is not short on restaurants by any means, but it is clear to see why Upland is constantly at full capacity in the spacious and airy dining room and why others who came late don't mind waiting.

Whenever possible the kitchen uses local meats and ingredients. We couldn't get enough of the bison burger. Part of that could be because the spent grain from the brewery is shipped off to a nearby farm and used as feed for the bison. The poultry also comes from local farms. There are plenty of great vegetarian options, including an outstanding white macaroni and cheese.

We enjoyed the community feel that Upland offers. Local artists display and sell their art on the walls. The brewery is involved with a lot of regional charities and recently began hosting a cycling event called Tour de Upland.

Upland has begun moving its product into other states, especially Wisconsin, but shows no signs of betraying its Hoosier roots for the sake of a buck. They recently opened a taproom and small brewery in Indianapolis (see page 88), giving residents of the big city a place to get growler fills and a fresh pint.

The Pick: Double Dragonfly Imperial IPA. A lot of breweries have embraced the double or imperial style in recent years. It's basically taking a recipe and cranking it up to the next level. Be it with hops or alcohol content. Upland has done both with his beer. Clocking in at 9.1% alcohol and 80 IBUs, the Double Dragonfly Imperial IPA is not for the faint of heart, but worth every sip.

Beers brewed: Bad Elmer Porter, Dragonfly IPA, Double Dragonfly Imperial IPA, Helios Ale, Preservation Pilsner, Upland Wheat Ale, Rad Red Amber Ale.

Upland Brewing Co.

Opened: 1998
Owner: Doug Dayhoff
Head Brewer: Caleb Stanton
Brew System: 37-barrel, 2-vessel JV Northwest.
Production: 6,700 barrels estimated for 2010.
Restaurant hours: Monday through Thursday, 11 A.M. to midnight; Friday and Saturday, 11 A.M. to 1 A.M.; Sunday, noon to midnight.
Tours: Saturday and Sunday, 3 P.M. to 5 P.M.
Take-out beer: Growlers, bottles.
Extras: Live music on occasion. Hosts several festivals during the year, including Maifest (spring), RadFest (summer), Hillbilly Haiku (late summer), Oktoberfest (fall), and Schwarztag (fall).
Special considerations: Family friendly. Patio is dog friendly. Handicapped- accessible.
Parking: Parking lot.

A WORD ABOUT . . .

Made in Indiana

Beer is far from being the only product crafted in Indiana. The state has scores of artisans and boasts a vibrant community of builders, confectioners, luthiers, artists, and makers of everything from engines to pickles.

These local artisans are well-worth seeking out on a trip through Indiana. Not only is much of their work unique and top quality, but they make excellent gifts.

In architecture circles, the state is known as the Limestone Capital of the World. Hard rock carved from quarries here built the Indiana Statehouse, the Empire State Building, Yankee Stadium, the Tribune Tower, and the Seattle Art Museum.

Indiana tops the nation in more eclectic exports too. What company provides more duck meat to dinner tables than any other? Maple Leaf Farms in Milford (www.mapleleaffarms.com). The Hulman Family of Terre Haute, in addition to owning one of the state's most iconic landmarks, the Indianapolis Motor Speedway, also runs one of Indiana's oldest companies, Clabber Girl Baking Powder (www.clabbergirl .com).

The Hoosier State is vital to the auto industry. One of the largest engine manufacturers in the world, Cummins (cummins.com), is head-quartered in Columbus, and radials from Hoosier Tire (www.hoosier-tire.com), founded in South Bend in 1957, have raced past countless checkered flags on tracks around America.

Indiana products are also important in the world of baseball. Sluggers Sammy Sosa and Rafael Palmeiro may have been tarnished by baseball's steroid scandal, but nobody doubted the quality of their bats, which were made by the Hoosier Bat Company (www.hoosier-bat.com) in Valparaiso. (We're assuming the corked bat Sammy Sosa was caught using in 2003 came from less upstanding makers.) Some other notable Indiana companies are Brandenberry Amish Furniture (www.brandenberryamishfurniture.com) and Clay City Pottery (www .claycitypottery.com). For readers who aren't beer purists, Indiana boasts more than thirty vineyards.

Hoosiers know how to eat as well as drink. Little Crow Foods (www.littlecrowfoods.com) in Warsaw has made corn products like Coco Wheats, Fryin' Magic, and Bakin' Miracle for more than a century. N. K. Hurst Hambeans (www.hurstbeans.com) of Indianapolis, established in 1938, is famous for its fifteen bean soups. Red Gold Tomatoes (www.redgold.com) of Orestes is known for its salsas and pasta sauce. Sechler's Pickles (www.gourmetpickles.com) in St. Joe has fifty-four flavors and hosts the annual St. Joe Pickle Festival.

And for dessert? Chocolate lovers will find their fix at the South Bend Chocolate Company (www.sbchocolate.com). Phylies still makes handmade candies in La Grange. And Mundt's Candies (www.mundts candies.com) in Madison has drawn raves from media outlets across the nation.

It only makes sense that a state famous for its corn would pop some. Yoder Popcorn (www.mundtscandies.com), started by Rufus Yoder in 1936, sits on a 1,000-acre farm in Topeka, while Pop Weaver Popcorn (www.popweaver.com), founded by Rev. Ira Weaver in 1932, is headquartered in Indianapolis. There's also Ramsey Popcorn Company (www.ramseypopcorn.com) in Ramsey. Poppers from miles around congregate in Valparaiso the Saturday after Labor Day for the annual Popcorn Festival, thrown in honor of the town's most famous native son, Orville Redenbacher.

Speaking of popcorn, everyone's favorite movie treat, consider for a moment all the movies shot in "Hoosierwood." A partial list includes *Public Enemies* (2009), *With Honors* (1994), *Rudy* (1993), *A League of Their Own* (1992), *Natural Born Killers* (1992), *Eight Men Out* (1988), *Rain Man* (1988), and, of course, *Hoosiers* (1986).

In that classic basketball film, the nonexistent town of Hickory stands in for Milan. That's just one example of the fictional Indiana towns seen on movie and television screens. NBC's hit sitcom *Parks and Recreation* is set in fabricated Pawnee, and the holiday classic *A Christmas Story* happens in made-up Hohman.

Many of the state's craftsmen say they draw their inspiration from distinctly Hoosier sources (For more Indiana-made goods, see www.visitindiana.net/madeinindiana.htm).

Brian Gordy, owner of Gordy Fine Art and Framing Company (www.gordyframing.com) in Muncie, was inspired to paint vivid watercolors of turtles after discovering the reptiles in the White River near his home.

"There's something about being in the middle of the country that makes the reasons for doing things rather genuine," he said. "When you have a critical mass of people in urban cities, the impetus for making art can be a financial one. In Indiana, that may not be a worthwhile motivation. It may even turn into a negative for you."

Many in Indiana are inspired by deep family roots. Peggy Taylor is a weaver who lives in her great-grandparents' farmhouse in Westphalia, where she raises sheep, fleeces them for wool, and weaves at a loom in front of the same window where her great-grandmother kept a quilt frame. "Textile creativity is in my blood," she said. "Could there be any better place to create than Indiana, where my family's craftsmen's lines converged?"

The combination of passion and heritage makes many Indiana crafts special. Chris Gustini, of Homestead Weaving (www.homesteadweaver.com) in Columbus, noted that residents and visitors alike appreciate things made in small quantities, or one-of-a-kind, made "by a real live artisan."

Lynn Retson, of Porter, paints roadsides of the state nicknamed the Crossroads of America. She draws inspiration as much from Indiana's residents as she does its scenery.

"I find there's something very democratic about it and very representative of the American spirit," she said. "We have strong agriculture, strong manufacturing, and more entrepreneurship with artisans and crafters."

Artist Joyce Jensen, of Zionsville, believes it's Hoosier institutions like the Indiana State Fair, the Indiana State Museum, the Indianapolis Museum of Art, and the Eiteljorg Museum of American Indians and Western Art that nurture the state's culture of creativity and industriousness.

"Indiana is a great place for creative people, whether a painter like me, a beverage or food artisan, or a craftsperson," she said. "There's room for new trends and old traditions." She added, "What could be more traditional than brewing beer?"

Guitar builder Clint Bear, of Madison, believes quality is more a matter of personal pride than state pride. But he concedes his state is blessed with a lot of folks with reasons to walk tall. "I think that's not unique to Indiana," he said. "Any artisan or craftsman takes real pride in what he produces."

Dorel Harrison, who makes handcrafted barn and house plaques in Scottsburg, reflected on all the fine products that come from Indiana: engines, artwork, blocks for our nation's most iconic buildings, food, and beer. And he reflected on his own work.

"It has to do with the talent you're given," he said. "And it just so happens that I live in Indiana."

A brewer couldn't have said it any better.

Uplands and Ohio River
Southern Indiana

The first thing people should notice as they head south from the northern part of the state is how the landscape changes. The pancake-flat fields yield to small hills and mountains that push from the ground towards the sky. It can turn a monotonous drive into a more pleasant one as you pass through rolling hills and thick forests.

This part of our journey takes us through Columbus, a city renowned for its collection of inspired public art and architecture. From there, it's off to Aurora, across from Kentucky on the banks of the Ohio River, as we follow the routes of old river traders south toward Louisville. Across the river from that city is New Albany, a town that has long lost people to the allure of the big city, but these days is rebounding and actually drawing Kentuckians back to Indiana.

Zip across the bottom of the state—through country that Abraham Lincoln once called home—to Evansville, a former factory town that has a growing arts scene and one of the better-known casinos in Indiana.

Most of this part of the state identifies with Kentucky. In fact it's known as Kentuckiana. But you can ignore the call from bourbon country and the annual derby, because while people around these parts might give their neighbor to the south the first half of a shared nickname, they know you do not have to go far to find something interesting or exciting.

There is also some great hunting and fishing to be had in this area, along with fun little towns where if you're into antiquing, you can get lost for hours.

Much of Indiana's historic roots can still be found in this part of the state, and it's a source of local pride. Folks proudly display furniture that was once made in the area or the appliances manufactured in industrial towns. We found people in this section of the state happy to talk about their ancestry and their own personal contributions.

While there have been hard economic times in the area over the last few decades, it's difficult not to detect the sense of determination and optimism in voices as these Hoosiers talk about the future.

Oh, and here's one important tip. A swath of southern Indiana—Daviess, Dubois, Gibson, Knox, Martin, Perry, Pike, Posey, Spencer, Vanderburgh, and Warrick Counties—operates on Central Time. It's an area that extends from Evansville east toward Santa Claus.

It's one hour behind Indianapolis and Louisville. Just be aware of this because we don't want you to get to a place only to find it doesn't open for another hour.

Lodging in the area: The Herman Leive House was once the home of Samuel Langtree, the master brewer of the Crescent Brewery. Today it's a charming bed-and-breakfast, just a block from the Ohio River, that is well appointed with locally made furniture (203 Fifth Street, Aurora, 812-926-0944, www.hermanleivehouse.com). LeMerigot Hotel at Casino Aztar in Evansville is a luxury hotel across the street from the casino and in the heart of a nightlife district complete with bars, clubs, and restaurants. One of the more modern hotels in the area, we found it to be a fun place to stay. 615 N.W. Riverside Drive, Evansville, 1-888-633-1770, www.lemerigotevansville.com. Holiday Inn Express is clean and within walking distance to the Bank Street location of New Albanian Brewing Company. 411 West Spring Street, New Albany, 812-945-2771. Also check with the convention and visitors bureaus: Columbus, www.columbus.in.us; Evansville, www.evansvillecvb.org; Clark-Floyd Counties, www.sunnysideoflouisville.org; Southern Indiana, www.southernindiana.org.

Area attractions: Even if you don't have a keen interest in history, the *Lincoln Boyhood National Memorial* (Route 162, Lincoln City, 812-937-4541, www.nps.gov/libo) celebrates the adolescent and teenage home of our sixteenth president. Abraham Lincoln was born in Kentucky and became famous as a resident of Illinois. But the man who would one day end the Civil War spent his formative years as a resident of Indiana. Today, the site is a living-history farm with re-creations from the period and mementos and historic artifacts from the young Lincoln's life. There is a fairly easy walking trail on the grounds and costumed interpreters who demonstrate life in the 1800s.

If you're looking for fun that's a little more modern, check out the town of Santa Claus. *Holiday World* (1-877-463-2645, www.holiday world.com) is a theme park with water rides and roller coasters. Or, if you're into Christmas any time of year, you can check out the *Santa Claus Museum* (41 North Kringle Place, 812-937-2687, www.santaclaus-museum.org) for everything related to Jolly Old St. Nick. You can even mail cards and letters from town and they will receive a Santa Claus postmark.

The only operational Landing Ship, Tank is in Evansville at the *USS LST Ship Memorial* (840 LST Drive, 812-435-8678, www.lstmemorial .org). LST 325, which saw action in World War II, is 328 feet long and weighs 1,625 tons. It's an impressive site and important piece of military history. Also in Evansville, the *Willard Library* (21 First Avenue, 812-425-4309, www.willard.lib.in.us) is home to one of the most extensive collections on genealogy studies in the Midwest. Opened in 1885, it is still used as a library. The *Evansville African American Museum* (579 South Garvin Street, 812-423-5188) focuses on local art from sculptors, painters, and other artisans.

Columbus has a lot of public art and all of it deserves your time. Best place to start is the *Columbus Visitors Center* (506 Fifth Street), where you can pick up a map and see a chandelier comprised of nine hundred pieces of hand-blown glass designed by Dale Chihuly.

Other beer sites: *Bourbons Bar and Grill* (1 East High Street, Lawrenceburg, 812-537-1221) has Great Crescent beers on tap. Their name lives up to their whiskey selection behind the bar. And then there's the coleslaw; it's thick and creamy, slightly sweet, with generous chunks of smoked bacon mixed in. *Lil Charlie's Restaurant and Brewery* (504 East Pearl Street, Batesville, 812-934-6392, www.lilcharlies.com) is not actually a brewery, because they only have fermentation tanks on the premises. But they pour decent beers and the food is among the best between Cincinnati and Indianapolis. At *Gerst Haus* (2100 West Franklin Street, Evansville, 812-424-1420), black and gold bunting hangs from most of the windows and Bavarian music is piped through the sound system. Their prices are reasonable and they have a decent craft beer selection served in unique glassware. Try the 18-ounce fishbowl. *Fourth Street Bar and Grill* (433 4th Street, Columbus, 812-376-7063) was recommended by our pals at Power House. We trust them.

Power House Brewing Company

322 4th Street, Columbus, IN 47201
(812) 375-8800 • www.powerhousebrewingco.com

He lived and died by the banks of the Flatrock River in a shack built for him by grateful parents of children he taught to swim in the waters that ran under his old home, a railroad bridge in Noblitt Park known as "Jack the Bum's Bridge."

A swimmer of surprising grace, Jack Miller, later "Uncle Jack" to his students and "Jack the Bum" to his immortalizers, was renowned for teaching youngsters how to paddle in those then-unpolluted waters. He even saved one boy from drowning.

Though he passed away in 1932 at the age of eighty-five, Jack the Bum still looks out at Columbus from a painting on the walls of City Hall. Below the words, "Childhood Friend" and "Storyteller," the painting shows a snow-bearded Jack, clad in an old-time swimsuit, holding hands with kids and standing in the water with Columbus in the background.

"I was drawn into the mystery of Jack," said painter Catherine Burris, whose portrait of Jack was dedicated in 1999. "He represented another time, and he's part of Columbus history."

Today Jack is also immortalized in another classic Columbus building, though instead of being enshrined in acrylic paint, he is celebrated in amber. Jack the Bum's Pale Ale, tart and hoppy, is one of the best-selling brews at the newly renovated Columbus Bar, home of Power House Brewing. "He's a character in our local folklore, and I want to keep things local," said Powerhouse owner and brewer Jon Myers. "I also thought it would be a cool name for a beer." When it came time to choose artwork to adorn the Pale Ale tap, Jon chose the visage of another famous vagabond, *On the Road* author Jack Kerouac.

Jon was a homebrewer whose family-owned Columbia Bar & Grill on the west side of town served craft beer. Talking with a regular one day, he fantasized about how cool it would be to open a brewery in the storied tavern. By 2007, Jon did just that, crafting the first beer of any kind in the

The Pick: Enjoy a pint of Jack the Bum's Pale Ale. It's tart and hoppy and would pass muster in California, where this style was perfected.

Beers brewed: Jack the Bum's Pale Ale, Wee Heavy Scotch Ale, Diesel Oil Stout, IPA, Working Man's Wheat.

establishment since it was a soda shop that made root beer during Prohibition.

The stainless steel brewing kegs sit in a small alcove next to the front door. When Jon brews he moves aside the nearest sitting booth and pulls the equipment out to mix the malts, hops, and grains. He brews early in the morning, so he can avoid disrupting the customers. To accommodate the brewing schedule, the bar does not open until 4 P.M. on Sundays.

Jon also brews a Wee Heavy Scotch Ale and a Diesel Oil Stout, named in homage to Cummins, a major employer in town that makes diesel engines. Jon also brews an IPA and the Workingman's Wheat.

The bar features taps with one of the state's widest arrays of craft beers, including Fade to Black, Oaked Baked, Black Biscuit, Double Trouble, Hopslam, Fat Tire, Belhaven Stout, Young's Double Chocolate, and Left Hand Milk Stout. The titles are written in red chalk on a blackboard that hangs above the bar's front door.

Like the namesake of its most notable beer, the bar itself figures in town lore. Built in 1939, just seven years after Jack the Bum passed away, the watering hole established itself as an institution in this factory town with a population of 40,000.

The neon sign that hangs outside the bar is the same one that has adorned the Columbus Bar's façade since its inception. John has focused on preserving the character and charm of the original bar, keeping the horseshoe-shaped bar itself, which was modeled after a streetcar and built in 1941. Two bronze plaques save seats for two men for their "years of faithful patronage." One is for Bill Burke, who has since joined Jack the Bum. The other belongs to Harold Hatter, 79, a retired Cummins architect who has been coming to the Columbus Bar every day for twenty years to eat the breaded tenderloin sandwich for lunch. His plaque commemorates his favorite seat.

"I always wanted to sit there; that was my spot," said Harold, who moved to Columbus in 1957. "I was like a milk cow in Kentucky always coming into the same stall to get milked."

The bar boasts a great menu and is known for its fried pickles. In the summertime they even serve hop-flavored ice cream. Hanging from the shelf encircling the bar are dozens of clear mugs emblazoned with the names of mug club members, who receive invites to keg tappings and free snacks on Fridays.

The high ceilings are white and made of pressed tin. The walls are yellow and covered mostly in large mirrors that give the room a spacious feel. There is a stage for live music on a second-story nook above and to the right of the bar, which is so high patrons chest-up rather than belly-up. Between musical performances, Nana Willey, a bartender, keeps the soundscape pleasant with piped-in songs by the likes of Todd Snider, John Prine, Robert Earl Keen, Son Volt, and Al Green.

Nana admits she is also responsible for many of the bumper stickers that adorn a refrigerator door just behind the beer taps. A sampling of slogans include: "My Bartender Can Beat Up Your Therapist," "Wish You Were Beer," "Protect Indiana's Waters," and "I Brew the Beer I Drink."

A Columbus native, Nana said she loves her job because of the people. "I have met some of the most amazing people that I wouldn't have met otherwise," she said. "The clientele here is just incredible."

The walls are decorated with old black-and-white photos of the Columbus Bar and the town itself. In a corner to the left of the bar is a bookshelf where patrons take and leave books as they choose. Jeff Jackson has been coming to the Columbus Bar since 1981 and worked there four different times under previous owners. He said the place had gotten shoddy and had fallen on rough times before Jon revamped it as a destination for serious beer drinkers."They've got the best selection of beers in town," Jeff said.

Jon said that initially some in town disliked the changes he brought to the old Columbus Bar. He quickly won them back, however, with reinforcements. "People who had lived in Columbus have come back in and said, 'Now it's really like it was in its heyday,' which is really cool."

Power House Brewing Company

Opened: 2006

Owners: Jon Myers, Doug Memering

Brewers: Jon Myers and David Baugher

Tours: The equipment is kept in a corner of the bar. You're welcome to take a look when you visit, but the bar is closed during brewing hours.

System: Home-brewing system that brews 20 gallons at a time.

Brewpub hours: Monday through Thursday, 11 A.M. to 11 P.M.; Friday and Saturday, 11 A.M. to 1 P.M.; Sunday, 4 P.M. to 11 P.M.

Take-out beer: Growlers

Food: American cuisine. "Fried to healthy," says bartender Nana Wiley.

Extras: Live music, open mic nights, poetry readings.

Special considerations: Handicapped-accessible.

Parking: On street or next-door garage.

Great Crescent Brewery

315 Importing Street, Aurora, IN 47001
(812) 655-9079 • www.gcbeer.com

Timing, as it is often said, is everything. In the case of Great Crescent, it took a little longer for Dan Valas to open his brewery, but when you visit today you'll see it was worth the wait.

The mid-1990s was a period in American craft beer history when a lot of homebrewers decided to go pro. They secured funding, found locations, and opened brewpubs or microbreweries. The country was awash in small-batch beer. It was difficult not to find a city or town that didn't have a brewery, and the media were filled with reports of this phenomenon. That helped drive customers, with cash in hand, to the establishments. Problem was a lot of these breweries weren't very good. Brewers quickly learned that just because their buddies enjoyed drinking their homebrew in the backyard, the concoctions weren't necessarily ready for prime time. A lot of them closed.

But many survived, either because of the pluck of their owners, generous funding from investors, or they were making quality beers that engaged a large following.

The craft beer scene remained still for a while. Some breweries would open, others would close, but there wasn't the same uprising of breweries that the 1990s had produced until about a decade later, when a new generation of homebrewers were buoyed by the successes of those who had survived and were celebrating decade anniversaries.

Dan Valas wanted to open in the 1990s, but he held off. In 2007, he realized that he still had the dream of opening his own brewery and began to act on it. In 2008, he opened the doors to Great Crescent Brewing. The name is a nod to the Crescent Brewing Company that operated in Aurora until Prohibition.

He opened in a storefront in downtown Aurora and demand was so strong, that he quickly outgrew the space. So Dan and his family set out to find a new home for the brewery. They first considered an office park outside of town, but real-

The Pick: Dan produced the Coconut Porter as a tribute to his wife, Lani, who is from Hawaii. Its nice malt flavor with slight earthy coconut tones make it a great beer for both a hot summer's day and a cold winter's night.

Beers brewed: Blonde Ale, Mild Ale, Stout, Coconut Porter, IPA, Cherry Ale.

ized they would miss the Main Street feel that they had enjoyed since day one.

Eventually they settled in a 47,000-square-foot warehouse that once served as a whiskey storehouse (the distillery was across the street). They have a cozy little storefront that serves as a tasting room, gift shop, and point of purchase for growlers and bottles of Sprecher's root beer.

The real allure of the new space, however, is down a small hallway, past a few offices and an impressive but nonworking wall safe. There is the old warehouse in all its aged glory. The ceilings are high, the walls are thick, and the place is built like a fortress. Dan pointed out a steel beam that was showing through the brick. It was imprinted with the number 77, as in the year 1877.

Aurora was once a big whiskey and beer town thanks to the T. & J. W. Gaff & Company, producers of bourbon, rye, and scotch who also owned an operation called the Crescent Brewery, famous for its Aurora Lager Beer.

Upon seeing the space and knowing its history, Dan found it just too good to pass up. Right now, it's a cavernous space, his tiny three-barrel system dwarfed by the size of the timber-framed room. He does have plans to upgrade in the near future to meet growing demand from residents and stores in the area. He also plans to open a restaurant in the space, having already met with architects and planning officials. Blueprints he showed off during a recent visit reveal what will likely be a great spot.

Meanwhile, he's already begun to assemble some equipment, including a grand mahogany bar that once belonged to an Aurora resident and some kitchen equipment he found on the Internet.

It's true that Dan waited a while to follow his dream, but for an area with a proud brewing history that has been without one for so long, it's better late than never.

Great Crescent Brewery

Opened: 2008
Owner: Dan Valas, Lani Valas
Brewer: Dan Valas
System: 3-barrel system.
Production: 100 barrels estimated for 2010.
Tours: Weekends and by appointment.
Take-out beer: Growlers available during business hours.
Special considerations: Handicapped-accessible.
Parking: Street parking available.

The New Albanian Brewing Company

PIZZERIA & PUBLIC HOUSE

3312 Plaza Drive, New Albany, IN 47150
(812) 949-2804 • www.newalbanian.com

The New Albanian Brewing Company is a bit Old World, with a dash of literary intrigue and a heap of revolutionary spirit. Or is it a Marxist dictatorship? One of the first things we noticed when we walked in was a framed picture of Chairman Mao. Then one of Vladimir Ilyich Lenin. This was a far cry from the sports banners or vintage beer posters that hang on many brewpub walls. But, wait, there's also a picture of Nelson Mandela, and one of Helmut Kohl, and one of Che Guevara.

All this makes sense once you meet Publican Roger A. Baylor, who is one of those guys who still uses the word "publican." A tireless intellectual and passionate citizen of the world, Roger has never brewed a day in his life, but he saw the potential in opening a brewery in this sleepy Ohio River town. It wouldn't be a brewery that served traditional beers, no. It would be a place where taste buds would be challenged, brain cells would be forced to work overdrive to comprehend the flavors and complexities, and a place where livers would hate their owners the next morning.

Situated in a pizzeria, once called and still often referred to as Rich O's Public House, New Albanian actually carried the name of a brewery for a decade before they brewed their own batch. A forward thinker, Baylor figured it would happen sooner or later and they might as well be ready with the name.

When they finally got around to brewing it was not the coup d'état of mainstream beer that the revolutionaries on the wall would have hoped for.

The Pick: Elector Imperial Red Ale. Not only because it's delicious, but we enjoyed the politically wicked way the brewery described it. We reprint, with permission, their description here: "Excessive hopping rendered moot a modest plan for brewing a traditional winter warmer, but the resulting hybrid was delicious and redefines the Imperial Red style category. The first batch of Elector was brewed on Election Day, 2002, a mere two years after the nation's electors (most recently) made democracy pointless, and we persist in thinking that an Elector in hand is worth two Bushes in retirement, any election day."

Beers brewed: You never know what you might find on tap, but here are a few good bets: Bob's Old 15-B, Community Dark, Elector, Hoptimus, Flat Tyre, and Mt. Lee.

The New Albanian brewers—Jared Williamson and Jessie Williams—are mavericks who brew everything from the extreme Imperial ales with high alcohol content to Prohibition-era beers that carry little punch but big flavor.

And while there are a slew of loyal customers who come for the beer, Publican Baylor regularly becomes professor and leads weekly classes where he teaches about various styles, pouring samples for his "students." It's an informal class, but for an area of the state that does not have a strong craft beer culture, every little bit helps.

Their guest bottle and draft list helps also. With more than three hundred varieties from around the world to choose from, New Albanian is quite possibly the best beer bar in all of Kentuckiana.

If all that wasn't enough to get you to visit, New Albanian is also home to Gravity Head, one of the country's more impressive beer festivals. It is a monthlong celebration of high-alcohol beers that range from the somewhat hard to find in the area to others that have been aging for upwards of five years. Baylor usually releases the list in advance, and once a keg or firkin is kicked, another takes its place.

Yes, other breweries hold festivals—daylong events, or maybe a weekend. A monthlong event is a rare treat for true beer lovers, *cerevisaphiles* if you will. This is surely an event and brewery not to be missed.

The New Albanian Brewing Company Pizzeria & Public House

Opened: 2002 (pizzeria, 1987; public house, 1990).

Owners: Amy Baylor, Kate Lewison, Roger Baylor

Brewer: Jared Williamson, Jessie Williams

System: Original equipment: 4-barrel Elliott Bay brewhouse with two 8-barrel Elliot Bay Unitank fermenters and two 8-barrel Elliot Bay Bright Beer/Serving tanks, circa 1996 vintage (previously owned by the defunct Tucker Brewing Company in Salem, Indiana). In 2005, the brewery purchased two 8-barrel DME Unitank fermenters, along with four 8-barrel DME Bright Beer/Serving tanks.

Production: 300 barrels estimated for 2010. Production of the core portfolio has shifted to Bank Street Brewhouse location.

Brewpub hours: Monday through Saturday, 11:00 A.M. to midnight. Closed on Sunday.

Take-out beer: Growlers

Food: Pizza, sandwiches, salads.

Special considerations: Handicapped-accessible

Parking: Building has its own lot. Additional parking across the street in the surrounding retail district.

The New Albanian Brewing Company

BANK STREET BREWHOUSE

415 Bank Street, New Albany, IN 47150
(812) 944-7112 • www.newalbanian.com

Drive by this place too quickly and you'll think it's a garage, not a brewery. Three glass bay doors face Bank Street in downtown New Albany, and in the warmer months, they roll into the ceiling and open the small dining room to the street.

It has a modern industrial feel to it, with high exposed metal rail ceilings, LCD lighting, and walls painted a strong shade of orange. But, what struck us most about this place was the width of the bar. Not the length. An l-shape with about ten seats, it's normal for a pub its size.

The bar is made from concrete and there are circular frosted lights imbedded into its surface, giving it the appearance of a lighted pathway, or something out of science fiction. The heat doesn't radiate through, and the 20-ounce pub glasses that they pour fit quite well. When the overhead light dims in the evening, the bar lights stay strong and highlight the true colors of the beer, making it like an aquarium where it's possible to see each little bubble happily float to the top.

The only art on the wall is poster-sized renditions of the beer labels, each drawn by the New Albanian artist-in-residence, Anthony Beard, who has somehow crafted modern drawings into a classic feel—part pinup poster and part Marvel comic book. All are worthy to hang in an art gallery.

This was the second New Albanian location to open—the other is about five miles away, also in New Albany. This one has more of a gastropub focus and a larger brewery where the guys can have a bit more fun.

The ever-changing menu is decidedly European, with dishes made from locally sourced ingredients that are undeniably delicious.

The Pick: Smoked beers can be hit or miss, but the batch of Cone Smoker we had was like bacon in a glass and kept us coming back for more. The secret, we're told, comes from putting the hops in the pub's smoker while they are making pork. Flavor is absorbed and translates well into the glass.

Beers brewed: You never know what you might find on tap, but here are a few good bets: Bob's Old 15-B, Community Dark, Elector, Hoptimus, Flat Tyre, and Mt. Lee.

It was warm enough when we visited, and the garage doors opened directly on to the sidewalk. It was nice to see passersby strolling outside waving to the bartender. It was also slightly amusing to see the men walking past with families who gave a lingering look of longing into the bar, before continuing on with their familial responsibilities. New Albany is one of those towns that has seen more than its fair share of hard times, and downtown especially has lost a lot of its nightlife to Louisville, which is directly across the river. The addition of this New Albanian location, however, is bringing people back—and even more from Kentucky into Indiana. Speaking of Kentucky—Bourbon Country—the brewpub has a wonderful selection of spirits along with the beer.

We met David Howard, a local homebrewer, while at the bar and he characterized the beer scene in Kentuckiana: "This is flyover country when it comes to beer—great beer on the East and West—but someone dropped the bomb and in the crater is New Albanian."

Amen to that. Every brewpub should be this great.

The New Albanian Brewing Company—Bank Street Brewhouse

Year Opened: 2009

Owners: Amy Baylor, Kate Lewison, Roger Baylor

Brewers: David Pierce, Jesse Williams

System: Custom-built DME Brewing Services 15-barrel, three-vessel Brewhouse, with four 30-barrel Unitank fermenters and two 30-barrel Bright Beer tanks.

Production: 496 barrels in 2009; 1,300 barrels estimated for 2010.

Brewpub hours: Tuesday through Thursday, 2:00 P.M. to- 10:00 P.M.; Friday and Saturday, 11:00 A.M. to 11:00 P.M.; Sunday, noon to 8:00 P.M.

Take-out beer: Growlers.

Food: Chef Josh Lehman sources and prepares locavore Kentuckiana foods and presents a constantly changing menu derived from continental influences, but showcasing microbrewing affinities.

Extras: Every Sunday from noon to 3:00 P.M. Louisville's original "build your own" Bloody Mary Bar. Live music during patio season. Annually in October (coinciding with New Albany's Harvest Homecoming civic festival, usually the second week of October), Fringe Fest, a celebration of local music and local beer.

Special considerations: Handicapped-accessible.

Parking: Small parking lot, soon to be supplanted for expansion of a beer garden. Street parking and surface lots surrounding.

Turoni's Main Street Brewery

408 North Main Street, Evansville, IN 47711
(812) 424-9871 • www.turonis.com

Look closely around Turoni's, a restaurant that encompasses three large storefronts on Main Street in Evansville, and you'll start to see images of Vinnie, a mustachioed, sunglasses-wearing, larger-than-life character who also happens to have a Jimmy Durante–sized nose. You'll see Vinnie with the Beatles and other celebrities and sports stars. "He's our Forrest Gump," said brewer Jack Frey "He's done everything, met everyone." The hand-drawn creation of local artist John Fiau, Vinnie has become the de facto mascot of Turoni's.

So when Jerry and Judy Turner and their family moved Turoni's from a previous location to its current spot on Main Street and decided to add a brewery to the mix, it seemed fitting that Vinnie should get his own beer. Vinnie's Lager is a light beer that goes extremely well with Turoni's thin-crust pizza.

Turoni's cooks their pizza in a bread oven and offers an expansive list of toppings. They encourage people to create their own circular culinary delight. Food snobs think that good pizza only comes out of Chicago or the New York City area, but Turoni's might just put Evansville on the map.

The thin crust is flaky but with a little chew, the sauce has just the right amount of sweetness, and the secret spice blend hand-mixed by Judy Turner in the office upstairs from the restaurant gives it an earthy aroma with some bite. When coupled with a pint of Vinnie's Lager, you have an all-American meal.

Vinnie, however, is not alone on the taps. There is the Blue Eyed Moose IPA, named for a moose head that hangs over the restaurant's gift counter. Turoni's legend is that Vinnie and Frank Sinatra hit the mighty beast with a car while on tour up north. Today, the moose has a speaker inside its head and will sing *Happy Birthday* upon request.

One beer that is not based on a fictional character, however, is the Ol' No. 23 Stout, named after

The Pick: Jack Frey doesn't make a bad beer, so you can't go wrong with any of Turoni's offerings. But, because one of the writers of this book roots for the Yankees (and there wasn't a beer named after a Cubs player), the Ol' 23 Stout gets the nod. Just be glad it doesn't cost $11 a pint like the beers at the stadium.

Beers brewed: Vinnie's Lager, Honey Blonde Ale, Thunderbolt Red Ale, Blue Eyed Moose India Pale Ale, Ol' 23 Stout.

hometown baseball hero (and should-be Hall of Famer) Don Mattingly, who played thirteen seasons for the New York Yankees while wearing the number 23. Mattingly still comes in from time to time, not only for the pizza, but to visit family—Judy Turner is his sister.

Brewer Jack Frey joined Turoni's in 2003 as an assistant after thirty years in the banking industry. He was promoted to head brewer in 2006 and has been consistently turning out well-crafted session beers ever since. Occasionally he will try something different (recently a few patrons have asked for a double IPA), but he mostly sticks with the classics. That's because while Evansville is many things, it is not a big risk taker when it comes to beer.

The big three corporate beers dominate in this town, where the most exotic beer you can get at the local casino is Blue Moon and most people are unwilling to try new flavors. I found this to be surprising since Evansville has a proud German heritage and there were once several breweries in town turning out expertly made German lagers, bocks, and wheat beers.

"These days Evansville is not a craft beer town," Frey told me with a shrug. There is a silver lining, however. The Ohio Valley Home Brew Club meets regularly around town sharing recipes and nostalgia and brewing batches for statewide contests. More importantly there is Turoni's, which is modestly turning out locally made beer for those who want it and converting others in the process.

Turoni's is a great-looking bar. It's only been open since 1996 but it feels like it's been around since your grandfather's time. Low lighting, an old jukebox, and advertisements from the earlier part of last century on the walls make it a place immediately familiar even to first-time visitors.

Turoni's Main Street Brewery

Opened: 1996

Owners: Jerry and Judy Turner

Brewers: Jack Frey, Corey Fisher

System: 7-barrel net system from Specific Mechanical in Canada.

Production: 650 barrels in 2009. 900 to 1,000 barrels estimated for 2010.

Restaurant hours: Monday through Thursday, 11:00 A.M. to 11:00 P.M.; Friday, 11:00 A.M. to midnight; Saturday, noon to midnight; Sunday, 4:00 P.M. to 11:00 P.M.

Take-out beer: Growlers.

Food: Pizza, sandwiches, and salads.

Special considerations: Handicap-accessible

Parking: On-site

Beerwebs

As the American craft beer movement has grown, so too has the number of websites dedicated to the breweries, beer, and the people who make it. Everything is out there, from sites that review beers one by one to those that provide beer and food pairings and detailed histories. It can be difficult to separate the wheat from the chaff, so here are a few of our own suggestions to help navigate the online beer world.

IndianaBeer
http://indianabeer.blogspot.com
This is the definitive site for news, gossip, and links regarding all things Indiana beer. Historian and beer lover Bob Ostrander is joined by a cast of others who get into the nitty-gritty of the Hoosier beer scene.

Hoosier Beer Geek
http://hoosierbeergeek.blogspot.com
Some of the most dedicated beer drinkers we've ever met run this fun, informative, and opinionated site. It routinely breathes life and personality into the act of drinking and is a must-read site for anyone planning on visiting Indiana and its breweries.

CraftBeer
www.craftbeer.com
The Brewer's Association, a group that represents the roughly 1,600 microbreweries, brewpubs, and craft breweries in the United States, runs this site, which offers profiles of brewing professionals, recipes and beer pairings, and news from around the brewing world.

BeerAdvocate
www.beeradvocate.com
This is one of the best places on the web for people to come together to rate and discuss beer. Opinions run the gamut at this site and can serve as a good introduction to a certain style or a definitive guide for a particular beer.

Seen through a Glass: Lew Bryson's Beer and Whiskey Blog

www.lewbryson.com

The man who wrote the first three books in the Breweries Series for Stackpole Books maintains a home on the Internet. It's clear to see why Lew Bryson is one of the most celebrated beer authors in the country. His writing is full of quick thoughts, well-rationalized arguments, and slices of everyday life. Visit once and you'll be hooked.

About Beer

http://beer.about.com

Our beer-writing colleague Bryce Eddings edits this site that includes news, thoughtful commentary, and links to all the doings in the beer world. A worthy read.

Holl's Beer Briefing

http://beerbriefing.com

This is a shameless plug for John's personal site, which includes musings and links to beer articles. It will also feature up-to-date listings of Indiana breweries that open and close after this book is published.

New Heathens

www.newheathens.com

Here's another shameless plug. This is Nate's chronicle of his band, the New Heathens; his fly-fishing trips; and anything else on his mind that day. He occasionally writes about beer and his deep love of the Rolling Stones.

Glossary

The following list of terms has been excerpted from the fourth edition of Lew Bryson's *Pennsylvania Breweries.*

ABV/ABW. Alcohol by volume/alcohol by weight. These are two slightly different ways of measuring the alcohol content of beverages, as a percentage of either the beverage's total volume or its weight. For example, if you have 1 liter of 4 percent ABV beer, 4 percent of that liter (40 milliliters) is alcohol. However, because alcohol weighs only 79.6 percent as much as water, that same beer is only 3.18 percent ABW. This may seem like a dry exercise in mathematics, but it is at the heart of the common misconception that Canadian beer is stronger than American beer. Canadian brewers generally use ABV figures, whereas American brewers have historically used the lower ABW figures. Mainstream Canadian and American lagers are approximately equal in strength. Just to confuse the issue further, most American microbreweries use ABV figures. This is very important if you're trying to keep a handle on how much alcohol you're consuming. If you know how much Bud (at roughly 5 percent ABV) you can safely consume, you can extrapolate from there. Learn your limits . . . before you hit them.

Adjunct. Any nonbarley malt source of sugars for fermentation. This can be candy sugar, corn grits, corn or rice syrups, or one of any number of specialty grains. Wheat, rye, and candy sugars are considered by beer geeks to be "politically correct" adjuncts; corn and rice are generally taken as signs of swill. Small amounts of corn and rice, however, used as brewing ingredients for certain styles of beer, are slowly gaining acceptance in craft-brewing circles. Try to keep an open mind.

Ale. The generic term for warm-fermented beers.

ATTTB. The federal Alcohol and Tobacco Tax and Trade Bureau, formerly part of the ATF, a branch of the Treasury Department. The ATTTB is the federal regulatory arm for the brewing industry. It has to inspect every brewery before it opens, approve every label before it is used, and approve all packaging. The ATTTB is also the body responsible for the fact that while every food, even bottled water, *must* have a nutritional information label, beer (and wine and cider and spirits) is *not allowed* to have one, even though it is a significant source of calories, carbohydrates, and in the case of unfiltered beers, B vitamins and protein. The bureau has become much more cooperative with the craft beer industry, presumably because they've recognized that it's not going away.

Barley. A wonderfully apt grain for brewing beer. Barley grows well in relatively marginal soils and climates. It has no significant gluten content, which makes it unsuitable for baking bread and thereby limits market competition for brewers buying the grain. Its husk serves as a very efficient filter at the end of the mashing process. And it makes beer that tastes really, really good. The grain's kernels, or corns, are the source of the name "John Barleycorn," a traditional personification of barley or beer.

Barrel. A traditional measure of beer volume equal to 31 U.S. gallons. The most common containers of draft beer in the United States are half and quarter barrels, or kegs, at 15.5 gallons and 7.75 gallons, respectively, though the one-sixth-barrel kegs (about 5.2 gallons), known as sixtels, are becoming popular with microbrewers.

Beer. A fermented beverage brewed from grain, generally malted barley. "Beer" covers a variety of beverages, including ales and lagers, stouts and bocks, porters and pilsners, lambics and altbiers, cream ale, Kölsch, wheat beer, and a whole lot more.

Beer geek. A person who takes beer a little more seriously than does the average person. Lew Bryson has been chided for using the term "geek" here, but he hasn't found another one he likes, so our apologies to those who object. Often homebrewers, beer geeks love to argue with other beer geeks about what makes exceptional beers exceptional. That is, if they've been able to agree on which beers are exceptional in the first place. A beer geek is the kind of person who would buy a book about traveling to breweries . . . the kind of person who would read the glossary of a beer book. Hey, hi there!

BMC. "Bud, Miller, Coors." Shorthand—usually derogatory—for mainstream lagers like these three brands. This has been used by craft beer enthusiasts since before it was "craft beer."

Bottle-conditioned. A beer that has been bottled with an added dose of live yeast. This living yeast causes the beer to mature and change as it ages over periods of one to thirty years or more. It will also "eat" any oxygen that may have been sealed in at bottling and keep the beer from oxidizing, a staling process that leads to sherryish and "wet cardboard" aromas in beer. Bottle-conditioned beer qualifies as "real ale."

Brettanomyces, or brett. A wild yeast that is generally considered undesirable in a brewhouse because of the "barnyard" aromas and sourness it can create. However, brewers of some types of beer—lambic, Flanders Red, and the singular Orval—intentionally allow *Brettanomyces* to ferment in their beer for just those reasons. Some American brewers have embraced brett, and a small but devoted group of drinkers have embraced those beers.

Brewer. One who brews beer for commercial sale.

Breweriana. Brewery and beer memorabilia, such as trays, coasters, neon signs, steins, mirrors, and so on, including the objects of desire of the beer can and bottle collectors. Most collectors do this for fun, a few do it for money (breweriana is starting to command some big prices; just check eBay), but the weird thing about this is the number of breweriana collectors who don't drink beer.

Brewhouse. The vessels used to mash the malt and grains and boil the wort. The malt and grains are mashed in a vessel called a *mash tun.* Brewhouse size is generally given in terms of the capacity of the brewkettle, where the wort is boiled. A brewery's annual capacity is a function of brewhouse size, fermentation, and aging tank capacity, and the length of the aging cycle for the brewery's beers.

Brewpub. A brewery that sells the majority of its output on draft, on the premises, or a tavern that brews its own beer.

CAMRA. The CAMpaign for Real Ale, a British beer drinkers' consumer group formed in the early 1970s by beer drinkers irate over the disappearance of cask-conditioned ale. They have been very vocal and successful in bringing this traditional drink back to a place of importance in the United Kingdom. CAMRA sets high standards for cask-conditioned ale, which only a few brewers in the United States match.

Carbonation. The fizzy effects of carbon dioxide (CO_2) in solution in a liquid such as beer. Carbonation can be accomplished artificially by injecting the beer with the gas or naturally by trapping the CO_2, which is a by-product of fermentation. There is no intrinsic qualitative difference between beers carbonated by these two methods. Brewer's choice, essentially. Low carbonation will allow a broader array of flavors to come through, whereas high carbonation can result in a perceived bitterness. Most American drinkers prefer a higher carbonation.

Cask. A keg designed to serve cask-conditioned ale by gravity feed or by handpump, not by gas pressure. These casks may be made of wood, but most are steel with special plumbing.

Cask-conditioned beer. An unfiltered beer that is put in a cask before it is completely ready to serve. The yeast still in the beer continues to work and ideally brings the beer to perfection at the point of sale, resulting in a beautifully fresh beer that has a "soft" natural carbonation and beautiful array of aromas. The flip side to achieving this supreme freshness is that as the beer is poured, air replaces it in the cask, and the beer will become sour within five days. Bars should sell the cask out before then or remove it from sale. If you are served sour cask-conditioned beer, send it back. Better yet, ask politely for a taste before ordering. Cask-conditioned beer is generally served at cellar temperature (55 to 60 degrees Fahrenheit) and is lightly carbonated. Cask-conditioned beers are almost always ales, but some American brewers are experimenting with cask-conditioned lager beers.

Cold-filtering. The practice of passing finished beer through progressively finer filters (usually cellulose or ceramic) to strip out microorganisms that can spoil the beer when it is stored. Brewers like Coors and Miller, and also some smaller brewers, use cold-filtering as an alternative to pasteurization (see below). Some beer geeks complain that this "strip-filtering" robs beers of their more subtle complexities and some of their body. We're not sure about that, but we do know that unfiltered beer right from the brewery tank almost always tastes more intense than the filtered, packaged beer.

Contract brewer. A brewer who hires an existing brewery to brew beer on contract. Contract brewers range from those who simply have a different label put on one of the brewery's existing brands to those who maintain a separate on-site staff to actually brew the beer at the brewery. Some brewers and beer geeks feel contract-brewed beer is inherently inferior. This is strictly a moral and business issue; some of the best beers on the market are contract-brewed.

Craft brewer. The new term for *microbrewer*. *Craft brewer*, like *microbrewer* before it, is really a code word for any brewer producing beers other than mainstream American lagers like Budweiser and Miller Lite.

Decoction. The type of mashing often used by lager brewers to wring the full character from the malt. In a decoction mash, a portion of the hot mash is taken to another vessel, brought to boiling, and returned to the mash, thus raising the temperature. See also *infusion*.

Draft. Beer dispensed from a tap, whether from a keg or a cask. Draft beer is not pasteurized, is kept under optimum conditions throughout the wholesaler-retailer chain, and is shockingly cheaper than bottled or canned beer (each half-barrel keg is more than seven cases of beer; check some prices and do the math). Kegs are available in 5-, 7.75-, and 15.5-gallon sizes, and almost all are now the straight-sided kegs with handles. Kegs are also ultimately recyclable, with a lifespan of forty *years*. Do what we do: Get draft beer for your next party.

Dry-hopping. Adding hops to the beer in postfermentation stages, often in porous bags to allow easy removal. This results in a greater hop aroma in the finished beer. A few brewers put a small bag of hop cones in each cask of their cask-conditioned beers, resulting in a particularly intense hop aroma in a glass of the draft beer.

ESB. Extra Special Bitter, an ale style with a rich malt character and full body, perhaps some butter or butterscotch aromas, and an understated hop bitterness. An ESB is, despite its name, not particularly bitter, especially compared with an American IPA.

Esters. Aroma compounds produced by fermentation that give some ales lightly fruity aromas: banana, pear, and grapefruit, among others. The aromas produced are tightly linked to the yeast strain used. Ester-based aromas should not be confused with the less subtle fruit aromas of a beer to which fruit or fruit essences have been added.

Fermentation. The miracle of yeast; the heart of making beer. Fermentation is the process in which yeast turns sugar and water into alcohol, heat, carbon dioxide, esters, and traces of other compounds.

Final gravity. See *gravity*.

Firkin. A cask or keg holding 9 gallons of beer, specially plumbed for gravity or handpump dispense.

GABF. See *Great American Beer Festival*.

Geekerie. The collective of beer geeks, particularly the beer-oriented, beer-fascinated, beer-above-all beer geeks. The geekerie sometimes can fall victim to group thinking and a herd mentality, but they are generally good people, if a bit hop-headed and malt-maniacal. If you're not a member of the geekerie, you might want to consider getting to know them: They usually know where all the best bars and beer stores are in their town, and they're more than happy to share the knowledge and even go along with you to share the fun. All you have to do is ask. See the Beerwebs section for links to the better beer pages, a good way to hook up with them.

Gravity. The specific gravity of wort (original gravity) or finished beer (terminal gravity). The ratio of dissolved sugars to water determines the gravity of the wort. If there are more dissolved sugars, the original gravity and the potential alcohol are higher. The sugar that is converted to alcohol by the yeast lowers the terminal gravity and makes the beer drier, just like wine. A brewer can determine the alcohol content of a beer by mathematical comparison of its original gravity and terminal gravity.

Great American Beer Festival (GABF). Since 1982, America's breweries have been invited each year to bring their best beer to the GABF in Denver to showcase what America can brew. Since 1987, the GABF has awarded medals for various styles of beer. To ensure impartiality, the beers are tasted blind, their identities hidden from the judges. GABF medals are the most prestigious awards in American brewing because of the festival's longevity and reputation for fairness.

Growler. A jug or bottle used to take home draft beer. These are usually either simple half-gallon glass jugs with screwtops or more elaborate molded glass containers with swingtop seals. Lew Bryson has traced the origin of the term *growler* back to a cheap, four-wheeled horse cab in use in Victorian London. These cabs would travel a circuit of pubs in the evenings, and riding from pub to pub was known as "working the growler." To bring a pail of beer home to have with dinner was to anticipate the night's work of drinking and became known as "rushing the growler." When the growler cabs disappeared from the scene, we were left with only the phrase, and "rushing the growler" was assumed to mean hurrying home with the bucket. When Ed Otto revived the practice by selling jugs of Otto Brothers beer at his Jackson Hole brewery in the mid-1980s, he called them growlers. Now you know where the term really came from.

Guest taps/guest beers. Beers made by other brewers that are offered at brewpubs.

Handpump. A hand-powered pump for dispensing beer from a keg, also called a *beer engine*. Either a handpump or a gravity tap (putting the barrel on the bar and pounding in a simple spigot) is always used for dispensing cask-conditioned beer; however, the presence of a handpump does not guarantee that the beer being dispensed is cask-conditioned.

Homebrewing. Making honest-to-goodness beer at home for personal consumption. Homebrewing is where many American craft brewers got their start.

Hops. The spice of beer. Hop plants (*Humulus lupus*) are vines whose flowers have a remarkable effect on beer. The flowers' resins and oils add bitterness and a variety of aromas (spicy, piney, citrusy, and others) to the finished beer. Beer without hops would be more like a fizzy, sweet "alco-soda."

IBU. International Bittering Unit, a measure of a beer's bitterness. Humans can first perceive bitterness at levels between 8 and 12 IBU. Budweiser has 11.5 IBU, Heineken 18, Sierra Nevada Pale Ale 32, Pilsner Urquell 43, and a monster like Sierra Nevada Bigfoot clocks in at 98 IBU. Equivalent amounts of bitterness will seem greater in a lighter-bodied beer, whereas a heavier, maltier beer like Bigfoot needs lots of bitterness to be perceived as balanced.

Imperial. A beer-style intensifier, indicating a beer that is hoppier and stronger. Once there was an imperial court in St. Petersburg, Russia, the court of the czars. It supported a trade with England in strong, heavy, black beers, massive versions of the popular English porters, which became known as imperial porters and somewhat later as imperial stouts. Then in the late 1990s, American brewers started brewing IPAs with even more hops than the ridiculous amounts they were already using, at a gravity that led to beers of 7.5 percent ABV and up. What to call them? They looked at the imperial stouts and grabbed the apparent intensifier: "Imperial" IPA was born. While this is still the most common usage, this shorthand for "hoppier and stronger" has been applied to a variety of types, including pilsner and—amusingly—porter.

Infusion. The mashing method generally used by ale brewers. Infusion entails heating the mash in a single vessel until the starches have been converted to sugar. There is single infusion, in which the crushed malt (grist) is mixed with hot water and steeped without further heating, and step infusion, in which the mash is held for short periods at rising temperature points. Infusion mashing is simpler than decoction mashing and works well with most types of modern malt.

IPA. India Pale Ale, a British ale style that has been almost completely co-opted by American brewers, characterized in this country by intense hops bitterness, accompanied in better examples of the style by a full-malt body. The name derives from the style's origin as a beer brewed for export to British beer drinkers in India. The beer was strong and heavily laced with hops—a natural preservative—to better endure the long sea voyage. Some British brewers claim that the beer was brewed that way in order to be diluted upon arrival in India, a kind of "beer concentrate" that saved on shipping costs.

Kräusening. The practice of carbonating beer by a second fermentation. After the main fermentation has taken place and its vigorous blowoff of carbon dioxide has been allowed to escape, a small amount of fresh wort is added to the tank. A second fermentation takes place, and the carbon dioxide is captured in solution. General opinion is that there is little sensory difference between kräusened beer and beer carbonated by injection, but some brewers use this more traditional method.

Lager. The generic term for all cold-fermented beers. Lager has also been appropriated as a name for the lightly hopped pilsners that have become the world's most popular beers, such as Budweiser, Ki-Rin, Brahma, Heineken, and Foster's. Many people speak of pilsners and lagers as if they are two different syles of beer, which is incorrect. All pilsners are lagers, but not all lagers are pilsners. Some are bocks, hellesbiers, and Märzens.

Lambic. A very odd style of beer brewed in Belgium that could take pages to explain. Suffice it to say that the beer is fermented spontaneously by airborne wild yeasts and bacteria that are resident in the aged wooden fermenting casks. The beer's sensory characteristics have been described as funky, barnyard, and horseblanket . . . it's an acquired taste. But once you have that taste, lambics can be extremely rewarding. Most knowledgeable people believe that the beers can be brewed only in a small area of Belgium, because of the peculiarities of the wild yeasts. But some American brewers have had a degree of success in replicating this character by carefully using prepared cultures of yeasts and bacteria.

Malt. Generally this refers to malted barley, although other grains can be malted and used in brewing. Barley is wetted and allowed to sprout, which causes the hard, stable starches in the grain to convert to soluble starches (and small amounts of sugars). The grains, now called malt, are kiln-dried to kill the sprouts and conserve the starches. Malt is responsible for the color of beer. The kilned malt can be roasted, which will darken its color and intensify its flavors like a French roast coffee.

Mash. A mixture of cracked grains of malt and water, which is then heated. Heating causes starches in the malt to convert to sugars, which will be consumed by the yeast in fermentation. The length of time the mash is heated, temperatures, and techniques used are crucial to the character of the finished beer. Two mashing techniques are infusion and decoction.

Megabrewer. A mainstream brewer, generally producing 5 million or more barrels of American-style pilsner beer annually. Anheuser-Busch, Miller, and Coors are the best-known megabrewers.

Microbrewer. A somewhat dated term, originally defined as a brewer producing less than 15,000 barrels of beer in a year. Microbrewer, like craft brewer, is generally applied to any brewer producing beers other than mainstream American lagers.

Original gravity. See *gravity.*

Pasteurization. A process named for its inventor, Louis Pasteur, the famed French microbiologist. Pasteurization involves heating beer to kill the microorganisms in it. This keeps beer fresh longer, but unfortunately it also changes the flavor, because the beer is essentially cooked. "Flash pasteurization" sends fresh beer through a heated pipe where most of the microorganisms are killed; here the beer is hot for only twenty seconds or so, as opposed to the twenty to thirty minutes of regular "tunnel" pasteurization. See also *cold-filtering.*

Pilsner. The Beer That Conquered the World. Developed in 1842 in Pilsen (now Plzen, in the Czech Republic), it is a hoppy pale lager that quickly became known as *pilsner* or *pilsener*, a German word meaning simply "from Pilsen." Pilsner rapidly became the most popular beer in the world and now accounts for more than 80 percent of all beer consumed worldwide. *Budweiser*, a less hoppy, more delicate version of pilsner, was developed in the Czech town of Budejovice, formerly known as Budweis. Anheuser-Busch's Budweiser, the world's best-selling beer, is quite a different animal.

Pitching. The technical term for adding yeast to wort.

Prohibition. The period from 1920 to 1933 when the sale, manufacture, or transportation of alcoholic beverages was illegal in the United States, thanks to the Eighteenth Amendment and the Volstead Act. Prohibition had a disastrous effect on American brewing and brought about a huge growth in organized crime and government corruption. Repeal of Prohibition came with ratification of the Twenty-first Amendment in December 1933. Beer drinkers, however, had gotten an eight-month head start when the Volstead Act, the enforcement legislation of Prohibition, was amended to allow sales of 3.2 percent ABW beer. The amendment took effect at midnight, April 7. According to Will Anderson's *From Beer to Eternity*, more than 1 million barrels of beer were consumed on April 7: 2,323,000 six-packs each hour.

Real ale. See *cask-conditioned beer.*

Regional brewery. Somewhere between a micro- and a megabrewer. Annual production by regional breweries ranges from 35,000 to 2 million barrels. They generally brew mainstream American lagers. However, some microbrewers—Boston Beer Company, New Belgium, and Sierra Nevada, for instance—have climbed to this production level, and some regional brewers, such as Anchor, Matt's, and August Schell, have reinvented themselves and now produce craft-brewed beer.

Reinheitsgebot. The German beer purity law, which has its roots in a 1516 Bavarian statute limiting the ingredients in beer to barley malt, hops, and water. The law evolved into an inch-thick book and was the cornerstone of high-quality German brewing. It was deemed anti-competitive by the European Community courts and overturned in 1988. Most German brewers, however, continue to brew by its standards; tradition and the demands of their customers ensure it.

Repeal. See *Prohibition*.

Session Beer. A beer that is low to medium-low in strength, say 3 to 4.5 percent ABV, but still flavorful, designed for what the British call "session drinking," the kind that goes on all evening through tons of talk and maybe some snacks, and doesn't leave you knee-wobbling after 4 pints.

Sixtel. A new size of keg developed in 1996, holding one-sixth of a barrel: 5.2 gallons, or about 2.5 cases. Very popular for home use, and popular with multitaps as well. The beer stays fresher, and you can fit more different beers in a cold box. The word *sixtel* is of uncertain origin; it was not coined by the developer of the keg but apparently grew up among the users.

Swill. A derogatory term used by beer geeks for American mainstream beers. The beers do not really deserve the name, since they are made with pure ingredients under conditions of quality control and sanitation some micros only wish they could achieve.

Terminal gravity. See *gravity*.

Three-tier system. A holdover from before Prohibition, the three-tier system requires brewers, wholesalers, and retailers to be separate entities. The system was put in place to curtail financial abuses that were common when the three were mingled. Owning both wholesale and retail outlets gave unscrupulous brewers the power to rake off huge amounts of money, which all too often was used to finance political graft and police corruption. The three-tier system keeps the wholesaler insulated from pressure from the brewer and puts a layer of separation between brewer and retailer. Recent court rulings have put the future of the regulated three-tier system in serious doubt, which may spell paradise or disaster for beer drinkers.

Wort. The prebeer grain broth of sugars, proteins, hop oils, alpha acids, and whatever else was added or developed during the mashing process. Once the yeast has been pitched and starts its jolly work, wort becomes beer.

Yeast. A miraculous fungus that, among other things, converts sugar into alcohol and carbon dioxide. The particular yeast strain used in brewing beer greatly influences the aroma and flavor of the beer. An Anheuser-Busch brewmaster once told Lew that the yeast strain used there is the major factor in the flavor and aroma of Budweiser. Yeast is the sole source of the clovey, banana-rama aroma and the taste of Bavarian-style wheat beers. The original Reinheitsgebot of 1516 made no mention of yeast; it hadn't been discovered yet. Early brewing depended on a variety of sources for yeast: adding a starter from the previous batch of beer; exposing the wort to the wild yeasts carried on the open air (a method still used for Belgian lambic beers); always using the same vats for fermentation (yeast would cling to cracks and pores in the wood); or stirring the beer with a "magic stick" (which had the dormant yeast from the last batch dried on its surface). British brewers called the turbulent, billowing foam on fermenting beer *goddesgood*—"God is good"—because the foam meant that the predictable magic of the yeast was making beer. Amen.

Zwickel. A *zwickel* ("tzVICK-el") is a little spout coming off the side of a beer tank that allows the brewer to sample the maturing beer in small amounts; it is also sometimes called a "pigtail." If you're lucky, your tour will include an unfiltered sample of beer tapped directly from the tank through this little spout. Some brewers are touchy about this, as the zwickel is a potential site for infection, but with proper care, it's perfectly harmless to "tickle the zwickel." It's delicious, too: Unfiltered beer is the hot ticket.

Index

About Beer, 126
Abston family, x–xi
ABV/ABW (alcohol by volume/
    alcohol by weight), 127
Action Duckpin Bowl (Indianapolis),
    71
adjunct, 127
African American Museum
    (Evansville), 113
Alcatraz Brewing Company
    (Indianapolis), 76–77
ale, 127
Anchor Brewing, 2–3
Anderson, Will, 135
Anderson's Vineyard and Winery
    (Valparaiso), 17
Anheuser–Busch, 2, 7
    Budweiser, 135
    tours, 34
Atomic Bowl Duckpin
    (Indianapolis), 71
ATTTB (Alcohol and Tobacco Tax
    and Trade Bureau), 127–28
Auburn
    Mad Anthony Tap Room, 17
August Schell, 136
Aurora, 111
    Great Crescent Brewery, 117–18

"Back Home Again in Indiana"
    (song), 1
Back Road Brewery (La Porte),
    28–30
Bailly Homestead (Porter), 17
barley, 128
Barley Island Brewing Company
    (Indianapolis & Noblesville),
    5, 11, 51–52
barrel, 128

Batesville, Lil' Charlie's Restaurant
    and Brewery, 11, 113
Baylor, Roger A., foreword by, ix–xi
Bear, Clint, 109
Bee Creek Brewery (Brazil), 11
Bee Creek Farm (Brazil), 38
beer, 128
    ale, 127
    ESB (Extra Special Bitter), 131
    IPA (India Pale Ale), 133
    lager, 134
    pilsner, 135
    session, 136
beer brewing, see brewing
beer geek, 128
Beer Geeks Pub (Highland), 18
BeerAdvocate, 125
Berghoff Brothers, 7
Berne, 39
Best's Brewing Company, 2
The Bier Brewery and Taproom
    (Indianapolis), 94–95
Big Woods Brewing Company
    (Nashville), 53–55
BJ's Restaurant and Brewhouse
    (Greenwood), 11, 38
Black Sparrow (Lafayette), 40
Black Swan Brewpub (Plainfield),
    61–63
Blackhorn Golf Club (South Bend), 16
Bloomington, 99–100
    area attractions, 100–1
    beer sites, 101–6
    Bloomington Brewing Company, x
    Crazy Horse Food and Drink
        Emporium, 101
    Irish Lion Restaurant and Pub, 101
    Lennie's/Bloomington Brewing
        Company, 102–4

lodging, 100
Max's Place, 101
Nick's English Hut, 101
Oliver Winery, 100
Scotty's Brewhouse, 89, 101
Upland Brewing Co., 104–6
Yogis Grill & Bar, 101
Bloomington Brewing Company
(Bloomington), x
BMC (Bud, Miller, Coors), 128
Bone Dry Bar & Grill (Highland), 18
Boston Beer Company, 135
tours, 34–35
Boswell, Ezra, 5, 8
bottle-conditioned, 128–29
Bourbons Bar and Grill
(Lawrenceburg), 113
Brandenberry Amish Furniture
company, 107
Brazil
Bee Creek Brewery, 11
Bee Creek Farm, 38
Brettanomyces (brett), 129
brewer, 129
breweriana, 129
breweries
location of, 12–13
micro, 9
regional, 135–36
tours of, 14, 34–35
visiting, 14
The Brewer's Association, 125
brewhouse, 129
brewing
history of, 1–9
home, 3, 67, 132
ingredients, 66
process, 66–67
terms, 127–37
brewpubs, 9, 129
Brick Road Brewing Company, 28
Brickworks Brewery (Hobart), 8–9
Broad Ripple
Barley Island Brewing Company,
11
Vigo Brewing, 11–14
Broad Ripple Brewpub (Indianapolis), 7, 8, 70, 72, 82–84, 91
Broad Ripple Brewing Company,
x, xi, 45

Broken Wagon Bison Farm
(Hobart), 17
Brugge Brasserie (Indianapolis),
xi, 72, 74–75
Bryson, Lew, 126, 127, 132
Buffalo Wild Wings (La Porte), 17

C. F. Schmidt Brewing Company, 5
CAMRA (CAMpaign for Real Ale),
129
carbonation, 129
cask, 130
cask-conditioned beer, 130
Centerville brewery, 6
Centlivre Brewing Company, 7
Central Indiana, 37–38
area attractions, 39
brew sites, 40–65
lodging, 38–39
Central Time, counties that operate
on, 112
Cephas Hawks brewery, 5
Champagne Velvet, 8
Charles C. Deam Wilderness Area
(Bloomington), 100
Chellberg Farm (Porter), 17
The Children's Museum of
Indianapolis, 71
Chumley's (Lafayette), 40
Chustak Public Fishing Area (Salt
Creek), 17
Circle Centre Mall (Indianapolis), 69
CKS Railroad (Knightstown), 39
Clabber Girl Baking Powder
company, 107
The Clabber Girl Museum (Terre
Haute), 39
Clay City Pottery, 107
Coffee Creek Park (Chesterton), 16
cold filtering, 130
College Football Hall of Fame (South
Bend), 16
Columbus, 111
Fourth Street Bar and Grill, 113
Power House Brewing Company,
8, 91, 114–16
Columbus Visitors Center,
Columbus, 113
Conseco Fieldhouse, Indianapolis,
71

contract brewer, 130
Coors Brewing, 7
Coster, Tom, 8–9
craft brewer, 130
craft breweries, 9
CraftBeer, 125
Crazy Horse Food and Drink
    Emporium (Bloomington), 101
Crescent Brewing Company, 117, 118
Crown Brewing (Crown Point), 1,
    18–21
Crown Point
    Crown Brewing, 1, 18–21
Cummins engine manufacturing, 107

DeBrand Chocolatier (Fort Wayne),
    39
decoction, 130
Dogfish Head Craft Brewed Ales, 4
    tours, 35
draft, 131
dry-hopping, 131
Dunns Bridge County Park (North
    Judson), 17

Eddings, Bryce, 126
Elkhart
    Mad Anthony's Old State
        Alehouse, 17
    Mishawaka Brewing Company,
        24–25, 45
ESB (Extra Special Bitter), 131
esters, 131
Evansville, 111
    Turoni's Main Street Brewery,
        x, 123–24
extract brewing, 11

F. W. Cook brewery, 5
fermentation, 131
The Fickle Peach (Muncie), 40
Figure Eight Brewing (Valparaiso),
    26–27
final gravity, see gravity
Firefighters Museum (Fort Wayne),
    39
firkin, 131
Fishers
    Ram Restaurant & Brewery, 11,
        38, 78

Flat12 Bierwerks (Indianapolis),
    92–94
Foellinger–Freimann Botanical
    Conservatory (Fort Wayne), 39
Fort Wayne, 37–38
    J K O'Donnell's, 40
    Mad Anthony Brewing Company,
        43–45
Fourth Street Bar and Grill
    (Columbus), 113
From Beer to Eternity (Anderson),
    135

G. Heileman Brewing Compnay, 7
geekerie, 131
Geneaology Center (Fort Wayne), 39
German Beer Purity Law, 67
Gerst Haus (Evansville), 113
Gordy, Brian, 108–9
Gordy Fine Art and Framing
    Company, 108
grains, 66
Granite City Food and Brewery, 11
gravity, 131–32
Great American Beer Festival
    (GABF), 132
Great Crescent Brewery (Aurora),
    117–18
Greenwood
    BJ's Restaurant and Brewhouse,
        11, 38
    Oaken Barrel Brewing Company,
        60–61
growler, 132
guest taps/guest beers, 132
Gustini, Chris, 109

Half Moon Restaurant & Brewery
    (Kokomo), 7, 8, 48–51
Hall of Fame Museum (Indianapolis),
    71
handpump, 132
Harrison, Dorel, 109
Heorot (Muncie), x, 65
Highland
    Beer Geeks Pub, 18
    Bone Dry Bar & Grill, 18
Highland Park (Kokomo), 37
Hill, John, 7–8
History Center (Fort Wayne), 39

Hobart
  Brickworks Brewery, 8–9
Hoham/Klinghammer brewery, 5
Holiday World (Santa Claus), 113
Holl, John, 126
Holl's Beer Briefing, 126
Home Brewery, 7
homebrewing, 3, 67, 132
Homestead Weaving company, 109
Hoosier, origins of nickname, 96–97
Hoosier Bat Company, 107
Hoosier Beer Geek, 125
Hoosier Tire company, 107
Hop-O beverage, 6
hops, 66, 132–33
Huntington, Quayle Vice Presidential Learning Center, 39

IBU (International Bittering Unit), 133
imperial, 133
Indiana
  artisans and crafters in, 107, 109
  companies in, 107–9
  counties that operate on Central Time in, 112
  known as Limestone Capital of the World, 107
  movies shot in, 108
  vineyards in, 107
Indiana Basketball Hall of Fame (New Castle), 39
Indiana breweries, 1
  history of, 4–9
Indiana Distilling Company, 7
Indiana Dunes National Lakeshore, 15–16
Indiana Dunes State Park, 15–16
Indiana Geological Society (Bloomington), 101
Indiana State Museum (Indianapolis), 71
Indiana Statehouse (Indianapolis), 70
Indiana University (Bloomington), 100
Indiana University Art Museum (Bloomington), 100–1
Indiana War Memorial (Indianapolis), 70

IndianaBeer, 125
Indianapolis, 69–71
  Alcatraz Brewing Company, 76–77
  area attractions, 71–72
  Barley Island Brewing Company, 5
  beer sites, 72–95
  The Bier Brewery and Taproom, 94–95
  Broad Ripple Brew Pub, 7, 70, 72, 82–84, 91
  Brugge Brasserie, xi, 72, 74–75
  Flat12 Bierwerks, 92–94
  John's Famous Stew, 73
  lodging, 71
  MacNiven's Restaurant and Bar, 73
  Plump's Last Shot, 72–73
  Ram Restaurant & Brewery, 11, 38, 76, 77–79
  The Rathskeller, 72
  Red Key Tavern, 73
  Rock Bottom Restaurant & Brewery, 1, 76
  Rock Bottom Restaurant & Brewery (College Park), 86–88
  Rock Bottom Restaurant & Brewery (downtown), 84–86
  St. Elmo Steak House, 72
  Scotty's Thr3e Wise Men Brewing Company, 89–90
  Sun King Brewery, 1, 8, 70, 80–82
  Tomlinson Tap Room, 73
  Triton Brewing Company, 91–92
  Upland Tasting Room, 88–89
  Vollrath, 73
  Yats Cajun Creole Restaurant, 73
Indianapolis Brewing Company, 7
Indianapolis Motor Speedway, 71–72
infusion, 133
Insomnia Cookies (Bloomington), 101
International Circus Hall of Fame (Peru), 39
IPA (India Pale Ale), 133
Irish Lion Restaurant and Pub (Bloomington), 101

J K O'Donnell's (Fort Wayne), 40
Jensen, Joyce, 109
John's Famous Stew (Indianapolis), 73

Kammus brewery, 6
Kankakee, 17
Koch, Jim, 34–35
Kokomo
    Half Moon Restaurant & Brewery,
        7, 8, 48–51
    The Quarry, 40
kräusening, 133–34

La Porte
    Back Road Brewery, 28–30
    Buffalo Wild Wings, 17
Lafayette
    Black Sparrow, 40
    Chumley's, 40
    Lafayette Brewing Company, 7, 41,
        45–48
    People's Brewing Company, xi, 8,
        40–42
Lafayette Brewing Company
    (Lafayette), 7, 41, 45–48
lager, 134
lambic, 134
Lawrenceburg
    Bourbons Bar and Grill, 113
Lennie's/Bloomington Brewing
    Company (Bloomington), 102–4
Lil' Charlie's Restaurant and
    Brewery (Batesville), 11, 113
Lincoln, Abraham, 112
Lincoln Boyhood National Memorial
    (Lincoln City), 112
Lincoln City, Lincoln Boyhood
    National Memorial, 112
Linebacker Lounge (South Bend),
    17–18
Little Crow Foods company, 108
Little Sheba's Restaurant & Zini's
    Place (Richmond), 40
Lucas Oil Stadium (Indianapolis), 71

McGinnis Pub (Michigan City), 17
MacNiven's Restaurant and Bar
    (Indianapolis), 73
Mad Anthony Brewing Company
    (Fort Wayne), 43–45
Mad Anthony Brewing Company Lake
    City Tap House (Warsaw), 17
Mad Anthony Tap Room (Auburn),
    17

Mad Anthony's Old State Alehouse
    (Elkhart), 17
malt, 134
    barley, 66
Maple Leaf Farms, 107
Martinsville
    Wilbur BrewHause, 55–57
mash, 134
Mass Ave Arts District
    (Indianapolis), 72
Matey's Restaurant (Michigan City),
    17
Max's Place (Bloomington), 101
Mease, Jeff, x
megabrewer, 134
The Melody Inn (Indianapolis), 73
Michigan City
    McGinnis Pub, 17
    Matey's Restaurant, 17
    Shoreline Brewery & Restaurant,
        8, 30–33
microbrewer, 134–35
microbreweries, 9
Mishawaka
    The Pub, 17, 25
Mishawaka Brewing Company
    (Elkhart), 24–25, 45
Monon Trail (Indianapolis), 72
Monroe County Courthouse
    (Bloomington), 99–100
Muessel Brewing Company, 5, 7
Muncie
    The Fickle Peach, 40
    Heorot, x, 65
Mundt's Candies company, 108
Munster, 3 Floyds Brewing
    Company, x, 1, 6, 8, 21–23

N. K. Hurst Hambeans company, 108
Nashville, Big Woods Brewing
    Company, 53–55
NCAA Hall of Champions
    (Indianapolis), 71
New Albanian Brewing Company, 6, 8
The New Albanian Brewing Com-
    pany Bank Street Brewhouse
    (New Albany), 121–22
The New Albanian Brewing
    Company Pizzeria & Public
    House (New Albany), 119–20

New Albany, 111
The New Albanian Brewing
Company Bank Street
Brewhouse, 121–22
The New Albanian Brewing
Company Pizzeria & Public
House, 119–20
New Albion Brewing Company, 3
New Belgium, 135
New Boswell Brewing Company
(Richmond), 8, 57–59
New Harmony Brewery, 5
New Heathens, 126
Nick's English Hut (Bloomington),
101
Noblesville
Barley Island Brewing Company,
51–52
Northern Indiana, 15–16
area attractions, 17
beer sites, 17–33
lodging, 16
sand dunes, 15–16
Norton, William J., 6

Oaken Barrel Brewing Company
(Greenwood), 60–61
The Old Bag Factory (Goshen), 17
Oliver Winery (Bloomington), 100
*One Pint at a Time: A Traveler's
Guide to Indiana's Breweries*
(Wissing), 9
Ostrander, Bob, 5, 9, 125

pasteurization, 135
Pennsylvania Breweries (Bryson),
127
People's Brewing Company
(Lafayette), xi, 8, 40–42
Peru, International Circus Hall of
Fame, 39
pigtail, *see* zwickel
pilsner, 135
pitching, 135
Plainfield
Black Swan Brewpub, 61–63
Three Pints Brewing, 63–65
Plump's Last Shot (Indianapolis),
72
Pop Weaver Popcorn company, 108

Power House Brewing Company
(Columbus), 8, 91, 114–16
Prohibition, 2, 135
fate of Indiana breweries during,
6–7
The Pub (Mishawaka), 17, 25
Public Enemies (film), 20

The Quarry, Kokomo, 40
Quayle Vice Presidential Learning
Center (Huntington), 39

Ram Restaurant & Brewery
(Fishers & Indianapolis), 11,
38, 76, 77–79
Ramsey Popcorn Company, 108
The Rathskeller, Indianapolis, 72
Red Gold Tomatoes company, 108
Red Key Tavern (Indianapolis), 73
Redenbacher, Orville, 108
Reinheitsgebot, 136
Reising, Paul, 8
Retson, Lynn, 109
Richmond
Little Sheba's Restaurant & Zini's
Place, 40
New Boswell Brewing Company,
8, 57–59
Robinson, Clay, x
Rock Bottom Restaurant & Brewery
(Indianapolis), 1, 76
College Park, 86–88
downtown, 84–86
Rogue Ales, tours, 35

St. Elmo Steak House (Indianapolis),
72
Salt Creek, Chustak Public Fishing
Area, 17
Santa Claus Museum (Santa Claus),
113
Schrick, Michael, 6
Schweber, Nate, 126
Scottish Rite Cathedral
(Indianapolis), 70
Scotty's Brewhouse (Bloomington),
89, 101
Scotty's Thr3e Wise Men Brewing
Company (Indianapolis), 89–90
Sechler's Pickles company, 108

Seen through a Glass: Lew Bryson's
    Beer and Whiskey Blog, 126
session beer, 136
Seward, Austin, 99
Shiojiri Niwa Japanese garden
    (Mishawaka), 16
Shoreline Brewery & Restaurant
    (Michigan City), 8, 30–33
Sierra Nevada Brewing Company,
    3, 135
sixtel, 136
Soldiers and Sailors Monument
    (Indianapolis), 69
South Bend
    Linebacker Lounge, 17–18
South Bend Brewing Association, 6
South Bend Chocolate Company
    (South Bend), 16, 108
Southern Indiana, 111–12
    area attractions, 112–13
    beer sites, 113–24
    lodging, 112
Southern Indiana Ice and Beverage
    Company, 6
Starlite Drive–in Theatre
    (Bloomington), 101
Stone Coast Brewing, 80
Studebaker Museum (South Bend),
    16
Sun King Brewery (Indianapolis),
    1, 8, 70, 80–82
swill, 136

T. & J. W. Gaff & Company, 118
T. M. Norton Brewery, 6
Taylor, Peggy, 109
Terre Haute Brewing Company,
    5, 7, 8
Three Pints Brewing (Plainfield),
    63–65
3 Floyds Brewing Company
    (Munster), x, 1, 6, 8, 21–23
three-tier system, 136
Tippecanoe Battlefield (Lafayette),
    39
Tomlinson Tap Room (Indianapolis),
    73
Triton Brewing Company
    (Indianapolis), 91–92

Turoni's Main Street Brewery
    (Evansville), x, 123–24

University of Notre Dame (South
    Bend), 16
Upland Brewing Co. (Bloomington
    & Indianapolis), 1, 104–6
Upland Tasting Room (Indianapolis),
    88–89
USS LST Ship Memorial (Evansville),
    113

Valparaiso
    Anderson's Vineyard and Winery,
    17
    Figure Eight Brewing, 26–27
Victory Brewing (Broad Ripple), 4
Victory Field (Indianapolis), 71
Vigo Brewing (Broad Ripple), 11–14
Vollrath (Indianapolis), 73

Warren Golf Club (South Bend), 16
Warsaw, Mad Anthony Brewing
    Company Lake City Tap
    House, 17
websites, beer, 125–26
Wells, Herman B, 100
Westchester Township History
    Museum (Chesterton), 16–17
White River State Park
    (Indianapolis), 71
Wilbur BrewHause (Martinsville),
    55–57
Willard Library (Evansville), 113
Wissing, Douglas A., 9
Wooden, John, x
Woodstock Inn, tours, 35
wort, 66, 136

Yats Cajun Creole Restaurant
    (Indianapolis), 73
yeast, 66, 137
Yoder Popcorn company, 108
Yogis Grill & Bar (Bloomington),
    101

Zevon, Warren, 14
Zorn Brewery, 7
zwickel, 137